The
Pharmaceutical Industry

Other Books of Related Interest:

Opposing Viewpoints Series

The Aging Population

Gateway Drugs

Health Care

At Issue Series

Do Veterans Receive Adequate Health Care?

Contemporary Issues Companion Series

Women's Health

Current Controversies Series

Prescription Drugs

Vaccines

"Congress shall make
no law . . . abridging
the freedom of speech,
or of the press."

First Amendment to the U.S. Constitution

The basic foundation of our democracy is the First Amendment guarantee of freedom of expression. The Opposing Viewpoints Series is dedicated to the concept of this basic freedom and the idea that it is more important to practice it than to enshrine it.

OPPOSING VIEWPOINTS® SERIES

The Pharmaceutical Industry

Jamuna Carroll, Book Editor

GREENHAVEN PRESS
A part of Gale, Cengage Learning

GALE
CENGAGE Learning™

Detroit • New York • San Francisco • New Haven, Conn • Waterville, Maine • London

GALE
CENGAGE Learning

Christine Nasso, *Publisher*
Elizabeth Des Chenes, *Managing Editor*

© 2009 Greenhaven Press, a part of Gale, Cengage Learning.

Articles in Greenhaven Press anthologies are often edited for length to meet page requirements. In addition, original titles of these works are changed to clearly present the main thesis and to explicitly indicate the author's opinion. Every effort is made to ensure that Greenhaven Press accurately reflects the original intent of the authors. Every effort has been made to trace the owners of copyrighted material.

Cover photograph reproduced by permission of Jonnie Miles/Photographer's Choice/Getty Images.

LIBRARY OF CONGRESS CATALOGING-IN-PUBLICATION DATA

The pharmaceutical industry / Jamuna Carroll, book editor.
    p. cm. -- (Opposing viewpoints)
    Includes bibliographical references and index.
    ISBN-13: 978-0-7377-4238-1 (hardcover)
    ISBN-13: 978-0-7377-4239-8 (pbk.)
    1. Drug development--Popular works. 2. Drugs--Research--Popular works.
    3. Pharmaceutical industry--Popular works. I. Carroll, Jamuna.
    RM301.25.P394 2009
    615'.19--dc22
                                                    2008034368

Printed in the United States of America
1 2 3 4 5 6 7 12 11 10 09 08

3 1000 00034 6612

Contents

Chapter 3: Are Pharmaceutical Marketing Practices Ethical?

Chapter 4: Is the Cost of Prescription Drugs in America Appropriate?

Why Consider Opposing Viewpoints?

"The only way in which a human being can make some approach to knowing the whole of a subject is by hearing what can be said about it by persons of every variety of opinion and studying all modes in which it can be looked at by every character of mind. No wise man ever acquired his wisdom in any mode but this."

John Stuart Mill

In our media-intensive culture it is not difficult to find differing opinions. Thousands of newspapers and magazines and dozens of radio and television talk shows resound with differing points of view. The difficulty lies in deciding which opinion to agree with and which "experts" seem the most credible. The more inundated we become with differing opinions and claims, the more essential it is to hone critical reading and thinking skills to evaluate these ideas. Opposing Viewpoints books address this problem directly by presenting stimulating debates that can be used to enhance and teach these skills. The varied opinions contained in each book examine many different aspects of a single issue. While examining these conveniently edited opposing views, readers can develop critical thinking skills such as the ability to compare and contrast authors' credibility, facts, argumentation styles, use of persuasive techniques, and other stylistic tools. In short, the Opposing Viewpoints Series is an ideal way to attain the higher-level thinking and reading skills so essential in a culture of diverse and contradictory opinions.

In addition to providing a tool for critical thinking, Opposing Viewpoints books challenge readers to question their own strongly held opinions and assumptions. Most people form their opinions on the basis of upbringing, peer pressure, and personal, cultural, or professional bias. By reading carefully balanced opposing views, readers must directly confront new ideas as well as the opinions of those with whom they disagree. This is not to simplistically argue that everyone who reads opposing views will—or should—change his or her opinion. Instead, the series enhances readers' understanding of their own views by encouraging confrontation with opposing ideas. Careful examination of others' views can lead to the readers' understanding of the logical inconsistencies in their own opinions, perspective on why they hold an opinion, and the consideration of the possibility that their opinion requires further evaluation.

Evaluating Other Opinions

To ensure that this type of examination occurs, Opposing Viewpoints books present all types of opinions. Prominent spokespeople on different sides of each issue as well as well-known professionals from many disciplines challenge the reader. An additional goal of the series is to provide a forum for other, less known, or even unpopular viewpoints. The opinion of an ordinary person who has had to make the decision to cut off life support from a terminally ill relative, for example, may be just as valuable and provide just as much insight as a medical ethicist's professional opinion. The editors have two additional purposes in including these less known views. One, the editors encourage readers to respect others' opinions—even when not enhanced by professional credibility. It is only by reading or listening to and objectively evaluating others' ideas that one can determine whether they are worthy of consideration. Two, the inclusion of such viewpoints encourages the important critical thinking skill of objectively evaluating an author's credentials and bias. This evaluation will illuminate an author's reasons for taking a particular stance on an issue and will aid in readers' evaluation of the author's ideas.

It is our hope that these books will give readers a deeper understanding of the issues debated and an appreciation of the complexity of even seemingly simple issues when good and honest people disagree. This awareness is particularly important in a democratic society such as ours in which people enter into public debate to determine the common good. Those with whom one disagrees should not be regarded as enemies but rather as people whose views deserve careful examination and may shed light on one's own.

Thomas Jefferson once said that "difference of opinion leads to inquiry, and inquiry to truth." Jefferson, a broadly educated man, argued that "if a nation expects to be ignorant and free . . . it expects what never was and never will be." As individuals and as a nation, it is imperative that we consider the opinions of others and examine them with skill and discernment. The Opposing Viewpoints Series is intended to help readers achieve this goal.

David L. Bender and Bruno Leone,
Founders

Introduction

"Many children ... have been put on medications without a thorough evaluation of family, school, and intrapersonal functioning, and are not receiving other, often-needed, therapeutic work, for example, to improve coping skills, family relationships, peer interactions, and/or schoolwork and learning."

Stanley I. Greenspan,
child psychiatrist

Just after Thanksgiving in 2001, Christopher Pittman murdered his grandparents in their sleep, set their house on fire, and fled in their SUV. He was just twelve years old. Diagnosed with clinical depression, he had switched his prescription antidepressant from Paxil to Zoloft a few days before the crime at his doctor's recommendation. His defense lawyers argued that the abrupt change in medication caused his violent episode. The Food and Drug Administration (FDA) has since required Zoloft and other antidepressants to carry warnings that they may be linked to suicidal behavior when used by youths. Though Pittman's thirty-year prison sentence still stands, many people have pondered the following question: Could prescription drugs be responsible for this adolescent's murderous behavior?

In the United States especially, where doctors wrote 11 million antidepressant prescriptions for children in 2002 and where an estimated 2 million to over 7 million children take drugs such as Ritalin for attention deficit disorders (ADHD/ADD), it seems important to determine the effects of mood disorder drugs on young people. On one side are pundits who declare that pharmaceuticals, and specifically mood disorder medications, are unsafe and unnecessary for children. Others, though, contend that such medicines greatly benefit the children who need them and are too often blamed for kids' bad behavior.

The main argument in support of prescribing drugs to children diagnosed with mood disorders is that when treated, they lead safer and happier lives. Young adults with untreated ADHD, for example, more often engage in risky behaviors, make more visits to emergency rooms, and are more likely to drop out of school than those who do not have the hyperactivity disorder, according to *FDA Consumer*. Conversely, when such children are medicated, those risks are greatly reduced. Young people with other mood disorders, such as depression, may withdraw from friends and family, lose interest in school, or become one of the estimated 500,000 teens who attempt suicide each year. For these reasons, some experts support giving antidepressants to children and credit the drugs for the decline in suicide rates in young people since 1994.

Parents who have seen the benefits of medication marvel at how their children's concentration, ability to learn, and performance in school improve. The mother of one boy relays that when her son was twelve, he was diagnosed with bipolar disorder and obsessive-compulsive disorder. She recalls, "He was placed on medications that address these disorders specifically. Within seventy-two hours, he had 're-connected' with reality, his moods improved and stabilized somewhat," and he re-emerged as the bright boy he once was. Toni Wood, who was not diagnosed with ADHD until she was thirty-eight, found that medication changed her life. "I saw such a difference. College was so much easier," she declares, and so were routine household tasks, such as paying bills.

On the other hand, detractors of pharmaceuticals allege that calming children down with medications stifles imagination. Many great thinkers, including Thomas Edison and Albert Einstein, are believed to have had ADHD. According to a

Wall Street Journal article, their creativity, exuberance, and penchant for daydreaming—and even their disorganization and forgetfulness—led to amazing insights and inventions. Robert Jergen, who wrote *The Little Monster: Growing Up with ADHD,* urges parents to help hyperactive children use their energy to be productive instead of suppressing it.

Cynics also charge that pharmaceutical companies promote drugs to correct behaviors that nearly all kids display and that do not require medication. Medicating toddlers with mood disorder drugs—in one case, a six-month-old was prescribed Ritalin for restlessness—is roundly criticized. In fact, extensive medicating has led commentators to dub younger people the "Ritalin generation." Edmund Higgins, clinical assistant professor of family medicine and psychiatry at the Medical University of South Carolina, opines, "Where I get concerned is when college students or even professionals come to me and say, 'I have trouble with attention.' Everyone has trouble with attention at some point—particularly with boring tasks." Higgins insists that people who display only some symptoms of ADHD must be separated from patients who actually have the disorder.

Another point of controversy is whether dosing children with prescription drugs predisposes them to drug abuse in the future. After all, some experts claim, it is only a matter of time before adolescents question why their parents give them drugs to calm them or make them happy but instruct them not to take illegal drugs for the same purpose. On a 2004 segment of *Online NewsHour,* Anne Taylor Fleming said of ADHD drugs and antidepressants,

> It's astonishing to think how pervasively these drugs have taken hold, how quickly we went from pot to Prozac, from a nation aghast at the use of drugs in the '80s to a nation encouraging their use twenty years later, even for the very young. . . . We should learn to live with our sorrows and griefs and ragged loves and losses, not treat them as

afflictions. . . . If we medicate our kids, they will not learn to manage their own moods and behavior.

Fleming's assertion is countered by those who proffer evidence that children on medications are *less* likely to abuse drugs later. For one thing, it is unlikely that young people will become addicted to the mood disorder drugs they are prescribed. Psychiatry professor Brian Doyle explains, "The vast majority of children and adults with ADHD are not using these drugs to get high but rather to feel normal. And if they're not chasing that high, they're unlikely to get addicted." Furthermore, though the mechanisms of action are not yet known, some research shows that treating children with ADHD drugs reduces their risk of future substance abuse. One review published in 2003 in the *Journal of Clinical Psychiatry* analyzed seven ADHD studies and concluded that ADHD-medicated kids are 50 percent less likely to abuse drugs later in life.

The disputation over prescribing drugs to young people illustrates how difficult it is to come to agreement on the appropriate use of pharmaceuticals. *Opposing Viewpoints: The Pharmaceutical Industry* explores multitudinous views in the following chapters: Is Pharmaceutical Research Safe and Unbiased? Are Prescription Drugs Appropriately Regulated? Are Pharmaceutical Marketing Practices Ethical? and Is the Cost of Prescription Drugs in America Appropriate? Though the people involved, from policy makers to patient advocates, all share the goal of protecting Americans' health, the reality is that the subject of pharmaceuticals rarely has unanimity.

CHAPTER 1

Is Pharmaceutical Research Safe and Unbiased?

Chapter Preface

One of clinicians' most critical tasks is to ensure that the development and testing of new medicines is safe and ethical. This is especially important considering the disastrous results of drug experiments on human subjects in the not-too-distant past. Before drug trials were regulated, some unethical experiments were conducted in which healthy people fell ill, patients' conditions worsened, or participants died.

One of the most flagrant examples of researcher misconduct was the long-term Tuskegee Study of Untreated Syphilis in the Negro Male. Beginning in 1932, the U.S. Public Health Service recruited over 400 black men who were not told they had a then-untreatable sexually transmitted disease (STD), syphilis. They were also unaware of the purpose of the study, which was not to find a cure but to investigate how the disease spreads, how it kills, and whether it runs its course differently in black men than in white men. By the time the experiment ended in 1972, a treatment for syphilis had been available for twenty-five years but was intentionally withheld from the study subjects. The researchers allowed the participants to die so they could see how the STD affects the body. Many of the men had spread syphilis to their girlfriends, wives, and children. Years later, President Bill Clinton formally apologized for "the lives lost, the pain suffered, the years of internal torment and anguish" caused by the unethical study.

Unfortunately, this was not an isolated incident. In another instance, the government sponsored unscientific experiments that were performed in uncontrolled settings by unqualified researchers. A secret Central Intelligence Agency (CIA) program, code-named MKULTRA, was formed in the 1950s to find a truth drug and other methods of mind control and brainwashing. As explained by Douglas Valentine in his *CounterPunch* Special Report, the heads of MKULTRA slipped experimental drugs, including the potent hallucinogen LSD, to vulnerable people. They targeted students, prisoners, soldiers, mentally ill patients, and prostitutes—those who were less likely to report the drugging. One man allegedly dosed Eliot Smithe's teenaged wife Barbara with LSD in 1953, without her knowledge or consent. Afterward, her mental health deteriorated. Five years later, she suffered a full-blown breakdown, characterized by paranoia and other schizophrenic symptoms that some doctors say may have been triggered by the drug. She was institutionalized for much of the next twenty years until she died. In 1980, after Eliot Smithe finally learned of the experiment, he submitted a $2,500,000 Claim for Damage, Injury, and Death against the CIA. His lawyers, though, could not prove that LSD had caused Barbara's breakdown. Also, because the MKULTRA records had been destroyed, little evidence existed to prove that she was involved in the program.

These stories present some of the most egregious and callous mistakes in scientific history. Though they did lead to stronger protections of human research subjects, such as patients' informed consent and research oversight by institutional review boards, these do not extend to participants of trials conducted by U.S. drugmakers in foreign countries even today. The issue of pharmaceutical research, therefore, remains a subject of controversy. As the authors in this chapter deliberate the safety and neutrality of pharmaceutical trials, they illustrate the great difficulty of conducting sound medical research.

*"'If those brave women hadn't partici-
pated in that trial, I wouldn't be alive
right now.'"*

Pharmaceutical Clinical Trials Save Lives

Jan Jarboe Russell

*In the following viewpoint, Jan Jarboe Russell extols breast can-
cer patients who volunteer for clinical drug trials, which she
claims extend their lives and helps researchers find a cure for
cancer. Because of people who are willing to participate in drug
trials, Russell maintains, clinicians have gained valuable insight
into the applications and side effects of experimental treatments.
As a result, she avers, new life-saving medications have been approved and cancer death rates have declined. Jan Jarboe Russell
is a writer and contributing editor for* Texas Monthly.

As you read, consider the following questions:

1. According to Russell, what was Dr. Fred Hausheer's explanation for why it is difficult to get new drugs approved?
2. What is the goal of Clinical Trials Task Force of San
   Antonio, in the author's contention?

3. What two claims does the author make about the drugs Bitsy now takes?

In 1998 Bitsy Brumage, one of my friends in San Antonio, had a recurrence of breast cancer, the same disease that had killed my mother five years before. Unlike my mother, Bitsy decided to participate in a clinical trial to test a new cancer drug she believed had a good chance to extend her life. I admired Bitsy's courage, so different from my mother's unwillingness to seek aggressive treatment: Mom wouldn't even consider seeking a second opinion, much less volunteer for experimental drugs. She was afraid of offending her doctor. To my mother and her generation, breast cancer was a death sentence. To Bitsy and women of my generation, it's a long-running emotional and scientific riddle. I think of these human volunteers who take part in clinical trials as the Good Rats—subjects in the great experiment to get new drugs and treatments out of the research lab and onto the market and, ultimately, solve the riddle of breast cancer.

Bitsy vs. Breast Cancer

The recurrence was a surprise—but so had been the original diagnosis. In the fall of 1992, Bitsy was only 44 years old and had no reason to see trouble coming, no family history of breast cancer. She and Max, her husband, had two sons, 9-year-old Jesse and 3-year-old Lee, who was the same age as my son, Tyler. One day Bitsy, who then worked as a psychologist at the Texas Headache Institute, in San Antonio, felt a small, fat lump in her left breast. She went to her doctor and within a few weeks had mastectomies on both breasts. The cancer had already spread to one lymph node. In the spring of 1993, she took six cycles of chemotherapy and a round of radiation. The prognosis was good: a 70 percent chance that the cancer would not recur in five years.

By 1998 cancer was no longer just Bitsy's disease; it had become her full-time job. She and four other women in her breast cancer support group organized the San Antonio affiliate of the Susan G. Komen Breast Cancer Foundation, which has contributed $3.2 million [from 1998 to 2005] for local services such as breast cancer awareness. But in April 1998, a week before the first Komen Race for the Cure in San Antonio and five and a half years after her original diagnosis, Bitsy experienced severe back pain. Her doctor ordered a bone scan. The cancer had spread to her lower spine. Nonetheless, on the morning of the race, Bitsy showed up early at Alamo Stadium, at Trinity University, to help register the 1,800 walkers, joggers, and runners and see them off.

It was Jesse's freshman year at Alamo Heights High School. He joined the drum line in band and soon became its star. Tyler and Lee were in the third grade, and that particular spring we were consumed with Little League tryouts. Many afternoons after school Bitsy and I sat in the stands at Alamo Heights Little League games watching our sons swing at balls, run bases, and catch pop flies. In those moments, buoyed by the sun-splotched green field and windy blue skies and the pleasure of observing our young sons at play, it was hard to believe that the world was not picture-perfect and full of life.

By then, several of Bitsy's friends had died of breast cancer. Some had participated in clinical trials both as a way to save their own lives and to help others. She resolved to do the same. Bitsy wanted to make meaning out of her cancer. It was personal: Bitsy versus the cancer. Even if she died, she wanted to have contributed to finding a cure for the disease. Dr. Fred Hausheer, a professor of medicine who specializes in oncology, spoke to Bitsy's support group and explained how difficult it is to get promising new drugs approved. The timetable is ten to fifteen years from the research lab to the market, and the average cost of producing a new cancer drug now approaches $1 billion. Research grants are hard to come by, especially if an experimental drug doesn't have obvious market potential. At this point, Bitsy was already undergoing more aggressive treatment—a strong form of chemotherapy (six cycles of Taxol) as well as an antibiotic and another cancer drug—but she worried that the treatment wasn't enough.

A Series of Clinical Trials

The leading center for cancer trials in Texas is M.D. Anderson Cancer Center, in Houston. In 2004 more than 12,000 patients participated in trials at the hospital, the largest such program in the nation. But Bitsy instead found a trial of a new drug at the University of Texas Health Science Center at San Antonio so she wouldn't have to travel out of town and be away from Max and the boys.

After gathering the information, Bitsy and Max sat the two boys down in the living room to explain the details. Bitsy told them that clinical trials were the only way that a cure for cancer would ever be found. The trials would allow researchers to gain information on benefits, side effects, and applications of new drugs. She described the research phases of trials. Phase I involves a small number of people and is generally the most dangerous. Patients are given a new drug that has never been used in humans in an effort to determine the proper initial dose levels. If the results are promising, the drug moves to phase II to determine more-refined dose levels and then to phase III, which involves hundreds, maybe thousands of people. The goal is to compare the new drug with the best-known drug on the market. Bitsy would be involved in a phase III trial of a new drug called Faslodex, an antihormonal treatment, to compare its effectiveness with Arimidex, the older, standard treatment. If Faslodex proved more beneficial, it would be considered by the U.S. Food and Drug Administration for approval.

Most people view clinical trials as a last resort. Bitsy saw her trial as a way to get better care and closer monitoring—not just by her own doctor but by the staff at the UT Health Science Center as well. Before the trial began, she met with

Clinical Trials Yield Information That Enhances Lives

Clinical trials are research studies that test how well new medical approaches work in people. Each study answers scientific questions and tries to find better ways to prevent, screen for, diagnose, or treat a disease. People who take part in cancer clinical trials have an opportunity to contribute to knowledge of, and progress against, cancer. They also receive up-to-date care from experts. . . .

There are several types of clinical trials:

. . . *Screening trials* study ways to detect cancer earlier. They are often conducted to determine whether finding cancer before it causes symptoms decreases the chance of dying from the disease. These trials involve people who do not have any symptoms of cancer.

Diagnostic trials study tests or procedures that could be used to identify cancer more accurately. Diagnostic trials usually include people who have signs or symptoms of cancer.

Treatment trials are conducted with people who have cancer. They are designed to answer specific questions about, and evaluate the effectiveness of, a new treatment or a new way of using a standard treatment. These trials test many types of treatments, such as new drugs, vaccines, new approaches to surgery or radiation therapy, or new combinations of treatments.

Quality-of-life (also called *supportive care*) *trials* explore ways to improve the comfort and quality of life of cancer patients and cancer survivors. These trials may study ways to help people who are experiencing nausea, vomiting, sleep disorders, depression, or other effects from cancer or its treatment.

National Cancer Institute, "Clinical Trials: Questions and Answers," May 19, 2006.

members of the research team, who explained the benefits and risks and told her she could leave the trial at any time. The cost was covered by her insurance company and the manufacturer of the drug. Once the trial began, she received one pill a day that was either Arimidex or a placebo and an injection once a month that was either Faslodex or a placebo. One of the two treatments had to contain an active drug. Naturally, Bitsy wondered if she was getting Faslodex. She and her research nurse, a friendly woman who never failed to ask about Bitsy's boys, speculated on it every month.

In October 2000 Bitsy's doctor and the research team found that her cancer had progressed again. She asked which drug she'd been taking: Arimidex, the old one, or Faslodex, the new? It turned out she'd been taking the old one. But Bitsy didn't give up. The following year, she participated in another small trial, and this time she got Faslodex. Not long after that, Faslodex was approved by the FDA. "I not only helped myself get new treatment, I helped get the drug approved," said Bitsy. "It felt really rewarding to be part of the solution."

Jerry's Story of Survival

By this time, Bitsy and Jerry Worden, one of the other founders of the local Komen Foundation affiliate, started a second organization, the Clinical Trials Task Force of San Antonio, to encourage both physicians and patients to participate in trials. Six years earlier, when she was only 39, Jerry had been diagnosed with inflammatory breast cancer, a rare and aggressive form of the disease. The first hint that anything was wrong was a tiny drop of blood from her nipple. A few mammograms later, Jerry learned she was in a late stage of breast cancer and had only a 15 percent chance of surviving five years. "I remember levitating," recalled Jerry. "I just mentally left my body. My girls were only four and six, and there I was, faced with an 85 percent chance of dying before either of them would be in high school."

After her diagnosis, her doctor told her the cancer needed to be attacked with repeated rounds of chemotherapy to contain it. Jerry balked. She wanted a mastectomy first. "I want the cancer out of my body," she told her doctor. The doctor showed Jerry the results of a clinical trial done in the early nineties at M.D. Anderson on women who had inflammatory breast cancer. One group of patients had chemo first; the other had mastectomies first. The group that had had chemo first had better survival rates. As a result, Jerry put off the mastectomy until after she had had chemo. "If those brave women hadn't participated in that trial, I wouldn't be alive right now," Jerry said.

Consequently, in 2000, Jerry volunteered to be a Good Rat. She was one of 5,187 women who participated in a Canadian-led international clinical trial for a drug called letrozole. Jerry had taken tamoxifen, the standard treatment for blocking estrogen to the tumor, for five years. After five years, though, tumors become resistant to tamoxifen. Jerry joined the trial at the Health Science Center. Like the other women, she received a pill a day—either letrozole or a placebo, because there was no alternative treatment. Two years later Jerry's trial was stopped early. Researchers had discovered that the women who were taking letrozole had a reduced risk for recurrence. Women who had been on the placebo were immediately offered letrozole. As it turned out, Jerry had been given the drug, not the placebo. Eleven years after her diagnosis and five years since the trial, Jerry's cancer is in remission.

Breast Cancer Is No Longer a Death Sentence

Bitsy's cancer continues to be what she calls "slow moving." In recent years, she has had both bone and liver progressions, which have responded well to treatment. All the drugs that Bitsy now takes were not on the market when she was first diagnosed, the year before my mother died of the disease, and all Bitsy's drugs have been approved as a result of clinical trials. If someone had told me thirteen years ago that Bitsy would still be alive and going to baseball games, band fundraisers, and Parent Teacher Organization meetings, I wouldn't have believed it. Jesse is in his last year of college at Texas Tech University, and Lee, like Tyler, is a sophomore at Alamo Heights High. Jerry's daughters, Kelly and Kimberly, are there too.

Between 1990 and 2001, the mortality rate for women with breast cancer declined by 2.3 percent annually. When my mother was diagnosed, breast cancer was indeed a death sentence. Now, thanks to people like Bitsy, Jerry, and the other Good Rats, the whole conversation has shifted from how to die of breast cancer to how to live with it. "Some people think clinical trials are an exercise in false hope," said Bitsy. "If you ask me, hope is hope."

> "Medical success stories mask a clinical
> drug trial industry that is poorly regu-
> lated, riddled with conflicts of inter-
> est—and sometimes deadly."

Pharmaceutical Clinical Trials Imperil Lives

David Evans, Michael Smith, and Liz Willen

*According to David Evans, Michael Smith, and Liz Willen in the
following viewpoint, people are too often injured or killed during
investigational drug trials. The authors allege that the Food and
Drug Administration (FDA), lacking resources to monitor drug
trials, allows research to be overseen by regulators who have ties
to the centers they are overseeing. Consequently, pharmaceutical
studies are poorly regulated, are run by unqualified researchers,
and include participants who are not aware of the dangers of experimental drugs, the authors contend. Evans, Smith, and Willen
are senior writers at the media company Bloomberg News, which
distributes information to business professionals.*

As you read, consider the following questions:

1. How many people in the United States have participated
   in experimental drug trials, according to Evans, Smith,
   and Willen?

David Evans, Michael Smith, and Liz Willen, "Big Pharma's Shameful Secret,"
Bloomberg Markets, December 2005, pp. 1–3. Copyright © 2005 Bloomberg LP. All
rights reserved. Reproduced by permission.

2. To whom has the FDA turned over its responsibility to oversee human drug trials, in the authors' opinion?

3. What is wrong with privatized review of drug experiments, according to Arthur Caplan in the viewpoint?

Oscar Cabanerio has been waiting in an experimental drug testing center in Miami since 7:30 A.M. The 41-year-old undocumented immigrant says he's desperate for cash to send his wife and four children in Venezuela. More than 70 people have crowded into reception rooms furnished with rows of attached blue plastic seats. Cabanerio is one of many regulars who gather at SFBC International Inc.'s test center, which, with 675 beds, is the largest for-profit drug testing center in North America.

Most of the people lining up at SFBC to rent their bodies to medical researchers are poor immigrants from Latin America, drawn to this five-story test center in a converted Holiday Inn motel. Inside, the brown paint and linoleum are gouged and scuffed. A bathroom with chipped white tiles reeks of urine; its floor is covered with muddy footprints and used paper towels. The volunteers, who are supposed to be healthy, wait for the chance to get paid for ingesting chemicals that may make them sick. They are testing the compounds the world's largest pharmaceutical companies hope to develop into best-selling medicines.

Cabanerio, who has a mechanical drafting degree from a technical school, says he left Venezuela because he lost his job as a union administrator. For him, the visit to SFBC is a last resort. "I'm in a bind," Cabanerio says in Spanish. "I need the money."

Turning Desperate People into Guinea Pigs

Every year, Big Pharma, as the world's largest drugmakers are called, spends $14 billion to test experimental drugs on humans. In the U.S., 3.7 million people have been human guinea pigs. Few doctors dispute that testing drugs on people is necessary. No amount of experimentation on laboratory rats will reliably show how a chemical will affect people. Helped by human testing, drugmakers have developed antibiotics capable of curing life-threatening infections as well as revolutionary treatments for diseases like cancer and AIDS.

These medical success stories mask a clinical drug trial industry that is poorly regulated, riddled with conflicts of interest—and sometimes deadly. Every year, trial participants are injured or killed. Rules requiring subjects to avoid alcohol and narcotics and to take part in only one study at a time are sometimes ignored by participants, putting themselves at risk and tainting the test data. The consent forms that people in tests sign—some of which say participants may die during the trial—are written in complicated and obscure language. Many drug test participants interviewed say they barely read them.

Ken Goodman, director of the Bioethics Program at the University of Miami, says pharmaceutical companies are shirking their responsibility to safely develop medicines by using poor, desperate people to test experimental drugs. "The setting is jarring," says Goodman, 50, who has a doctorate in philosophy, after spending 90 minutes in the waiting rooms at SFBC's Miami center, which is also the company's headquarters. "It's an eye-opener. Every one of these people should probably raise a red flag. If these human subject recruitment mills are the norm around the country, then our system is in deep trouble."

Pharmaceutical companies distance themselves from the experiments on humans by outsourcing most of their trials to private test centers across the U.S. and around the world, says Daniel Federman, a doctor who is a senior dean of Harvard Medical School in Boston. The chief executive officers of drug companies should be held accountable for any lack of ethics in these tests, he says. "The CEOs of the companies have to be publicly, explicitly and financially responsible for the ethical approach," says Federman, 77, who still sees patients. "It's not possible to insist on ethical standards unless the company providing the money does so."

CEOs of 15 pharmaceutical companies that outsource drug testing to firms including SFBC—among them, Pfizer Inc., the world's largest drugmaker; Merck & Co.; and Johnson & Johnson—declined to comment for this story.

SFBC Chief Executive Arnold Hantman says his center diligently meets all regulations. "We take very seriously our responsibilities to regulatory authorities, trial participants, clients, employees and shareholders," Hantman, 56, says. "We are committed to conducting research that fully complies with industry and regulatory standards."

The pressure pharmaceutical companies face to develop new drugs has intensified in the past 15 years. Faced with the expiration of patents on best-selling drugs like AstraZeneca Plc's Prilosec, which has helped tens of millions of people with heartburn and ulcers, Big Pharma has been in a frenzied race to find new sources of profit. When the patent for a company's blockbuster drug expires, a lucrative monopoly vanishes. Such drugs typically lose 85 percent of their market share within a year of patent expiration, according to Center-Watch, a Boston-based compiler of clinical trial data.

Government Oversight Is Inadequate

The U.S. Food and Drug Administration, the principal federal agency charged with policing the safety of human drug testing, has farmed out much of that responsibility to a network of private companies and groups called institutional review boards, or IRBs. The IRBs that oversee drug company trials operate in such secrecy that the names of their members often aren't disclosed to the public. These IRBs are paid by Big Pharma—just like the testing centers they're supposed to be regulating.

Animals Are Better Protected than Humans

"In many ways, rats and mice get greater protection as research subjects in the United States than do humans," said Arthur L. Caplan, chairman of the department of medical ethics at the University of Pennsylvania.

Animal research centers have to register with the federal government, keep track of subject numbers, have unannounced spot inspections and address problems speedily or risk closing, none of which is true in human research, Mr. Caplan said.

Because no one collects the data systematically, there is no way to tell how safe the nation's clinical research is or ever has been.

Gardiner Harris, New York Times, *September 28, 2007.*

The oldest and largest review company is Western IRB, founded in 1977 by Angela Bowen, an endocrinologist. WIRB, an Olympia, Washington–based for-profit company, is responsible for protecting people in 17,000 clinical trials in the U.S. The company oversaw tests in California and Georgia in the 1990s for which doctors were criminally charged and jailed for lying to the FDA and endangering the lives of trial participants. No action was taken against WIRB. Bowen says she didn't see human safety issues in those trials. WIRB aims to visit test sites it monitors once every three years, Bowen says.

The FDA's own enforcement records portray a system of regulation so porous that it has allowed rogue clinicians— some of whom have phony credentials—to continue conducting human drug tests for years, sometimes for decades. The Fabre Research Clinic in Houston, for example, conducted experimental drug tests for two decades even as FDA inspectors documented the clinic had used unlicensed employees and endangered people repeatedly since 1980. In 2002, the FDA linked the clinic's wrongdoing to the death of a test participant.

Problems with Privatized Review

Review boards can have blatant conflicts of interest. The one policing the Fabre clinic was founded by Louis Fabre, the same doctor who ran the clinic. Miami-based Southern IRB has overseen testing at SFBC and is owned by Alison Shamblen, 48, wife of E. Cooper Shamblen, 67, SFBC's vice president of clinical operations. Both Shamblens declined to comment.

SFBC's 2005 shareholder proxy, filed with the U.S. Securities and Exchange Commission, lists Lisa Krinsky as its chairman and a director of medical trials and refers to her 26 times as a doctor. Krinsky, 42, has a degree from Sparta Medical College in St. Lucia in the Caribbean; she is not licensed to practice medicine.

Arthur Caplan, director of the Center for Bioethics at the University of Pennsylvania in Philadelphia, says handing oversight of human drug experiments to private, for-profit companies is a mistake. "This whole world gives me hives, this privatized review process," Caplan, 55, says. "I've never seen an IRB advertise by saying, 'Hire us. We're the most zealous enforcer of regulations you could have.' People say, 'We'll turn it around faster. We're efficient. We know how to get you to your deadlines.'"

The FDA Cannot Aggressively Monitor Drug Trials

The Pharmaceutical Research and Manufacturers of America, a Washington-based trade association and lobbying group, says human drug tests in the U.S. are safe and well monitored.

"The vast majority of clinical trials conducted in the United States meet high ethical standards," PhRMA, as the group is known, said in a written response to questions. "The U.S. regulatory system is the world's gold standard, and the Food and Drug Administration has the best product safety record."

Joanne Rhoads, the physician who directs the FDA's Division of Scientific Investigations, says that view isn't realistic. "What the FDA regulations require is not any gold standard for trials," Rhoads, 55, says. The agency doesn't have enough staff to aggressively monitor trials, she says, adding that FDA regulations are a bare minimum and much more oversight is needed. "You cannot rely on the inspection process to get quality into the system," Rhoads says. "I know many people find this not OK, but that's just the truth."

Michael Hensley, a pediatrician who was an FDA investigator from 1977 to '82, says the agency has become less active in clinical trial oversight in recent years. Families of injured or dead trial participants seeking accountability for mistakes have to file lawsuits. "The FDA's backbone has been Jell-O," says Hensley, 60, who's now president of Chapel Hill, North Carolina–based Hensley & Pile Inc., which advises pharmaceutical companies on FDA compliance. "The folks at the FDA stopped enforcing the rules several years ago."

By law, drug companies must first conduct tests to determine whether potential drugs produce dangerous side effects, such as organ damage, impaired vision or difficulty breathing. The FDA calls them phase I tests. In 1991, 80 percent of industry-sponsored drug trials were conducted by medical faculty at universities, with protection for participants provided by the school's own oversight boards, according to the *New England Journal of Medicine*. Now, more than 75 percent of all clinical trials paid for by pharmaceutical companies are done in private test centers or doctors' offices, according to CenterWatch.

Improper Practices

Some test centers, FDA records show, have used poorly trained and unlicensed clinicians to give participants experimental drugs. The centers—there are about 15,000 in the U.S.—sometimes have incomplete or illegible records. In California and Texas, clinicians have used themselves, staff or family members as drug trial participants.

"Unfortunately, I don't think it's been recognized how important it is that people who actually conduct the trial be trained," Rhoads says. "We oftentimes see people with no qualifications whatsoever, but they'll go to a one-day training course and they call themselves a certified study coordinator." These people often run 90 percent of the study with little involvement by physicians, she says.

> "There is really no question anymore
> that there is a relationship between who
> funds a study and chooses the investi-
> gators, and the study's outcome."

Drug Industry–Funded Research Is Biased

Leonard Glantz, as told to Sara Hoffman Jurand

*Leonard Glantz is a professor in the Department of Health Law,
Bioethics & Human Rights at Boston University School of Public
Health. In the following viewpoint, he maintains in an interview
with Sara Hoffman Jurand, associate editor of* Trial, *that
drugmakers' clinical studies are biased in favor of their medicines. The results of drug trials sponsored by pharmaceutical
companies differ from those funded by the government, he claims.
In his contention, drug companies design studies, and hire researchers, that are inclined toward their product. Negative outcomes are rarely publicized, he adds, and trial results are skewed
because the subjects are mainly white men and not people of
varying ethnicities and ages.*

Leonard Glantz, as told to Sara Hoffman Jurand, "A Prescription for Better Drug Trials:
What Ails Drug Research Today?" *Trial*, vol. 41, no. 3, March 2005, pp. 54–58. Copyright © 2005 Association of Trial Lawyers of America. Reproduced by permission.

As you read, consider the following questions:

1. According to Glantz, what is the main purpose of drug companies' research?
2. What conclusion does Glantz draw from the study that measured hearing loss by two different hearing tests?
3. What drug does Glantz suggest is best at treating the pain of arthritis?

When a hugely popular drug like Vioxx is pulled from the market, or a black-box warning is added to the label of an antidepressant, many consumers wonder why these products' side effects were not detected earlier, before thousands of users were exposed to potentially serious harm.

The answer may lie in what many consumer and public health advocates believe is a dangerously ineffective clinical trial system. Too often, they say, a manufacturer's rush to market trumps concerns about patient safety, and limits on public access to trial data leave consumers and even government regulators ill-informed.

To improve the system, critics say, all drug trials should be registered in a comprehensive database at their outset. Unbiased research protocols should be developed. Results should be more available to the public. The benefit: more knowledge and greater safety for consumers. . . .

TRIAL: In your opinion, should there be a comprehensive database of clinical trial information?

Leonard Glantz: Yes. This idea is part of a larger effort to make data available so that people can interpret it for themselves. There's a proposal at the National Institutes of Health (NIH) that any NIH-funded research, when it's published, should be posted on a free Web site available to the public.

I think another useful idea is to have all the results of all clinical trials available on a free, publicly available Web site. This would be especially important for trials with negative outcomes, which tend not to be published, and for trials that have been discontinued before completion. When clinical trials appear to be heading in the direction of negative results, they may be stopped early and therefore aren't publishable. But they still may provide some useful information.

Should submission of data to the database be voluntary or mandatory?

Mandatory. . . .

How a Registry Will Make Bias Transparent

Until this proposed database is established, the International Committee of Medical Journal Editors has announced a new policy that clinical trials have to be registered in a publicly accessible database in order to be considered for publication in the committee's member journals—including the New England Journal of Medicine *and the* Journal of the American Medical Association. *Do you think this will be an adequate incentive for drug companies to register their trials?*

I think it will be an important incentive. Again, it remains to be seen, but I think it's a good start.

One thing that journal peer reviewers often don't know is whether an article includes all the available data about a drug. If an article reports on a trial that lasted 6 months, it's not clear if there's another 12 months' worth of information out there from another unreported trial. All reviewers can do is review what the authors give them from the 6-month trial, and the 12-month (unpublished) information may be quite different.

Having all trials registered and all the information available online would certainly help. And again, the concern really is studies with negative outcomes, which one rarely sees.

Do these proposals—both the medical journal policy and the idea for the comprehensive database—require researchers to divulge drug companies' financial support of research and any other possible biases?

I don't know if these proposals specifically deal with this area, but I assume so. Since these will be databases of drug companies' research, we will know who is funding it. Databases of NIH-funded research already exist. So potential bias will be pretty clear.

Lack of Diversity Skews Results

Last summer, an article in the Journal of the American Medical Association *reported that racial and ethnic minorities, women, and the elderly were less likely than white men to participate in clinical trials. What does this mean for the reliability of trials, and therefore for drug safety?*

Where there is a lack of diversity, the conclusions that one can reach may apply only to the specific group involved in the trial. It would be problematic for one to draw broad conclusions about safety and efficacy when the research included only a part of the population.

Last fall there was a lot of discussion about a particular drug regimen for heart disease that seems to benefit African-Americans more than it does Caucasians. This is a controversial issue because of the possible political ramifications of identifying race-based biological differences. But on the other hand, this finding demonstrates that different people—different genders, different ages, and different races—may react differently to drugs. When this is the case, it is an important thing to know so that the new drugs can be properly prescribed for patients in these different populations.

One thing to keep in mind about drug-company research is that its main purpose is not scientific. Its purpose is commercial: The goal of the pharmaceutical industry is to create products that can be sold. Often, underlying scientific questions—for example, Which populations does this drug work in?—are not explored. The issue for a particular company is, Can we get this drug approved? Once a drug is approved for any population or any condition, doctors can lawfully prescribe the drug for anything, for use by anyone.

It is useful and important to increase diversity in drug-company trials, so that the data can be accumulated and interpreted as it relates to different populations. The NIH has its own rules that require including different races and both genders in the research it funds.

What can researchers do to increase the diversity in clinical trials?

The FDA should consider requiring that medications be tested in a number of different populations.

The protocols for pharmaceutical-industry research are not created by the researchers who conduct the trials, but by the pharmaceutical companies. Those companies pay close attention to FDA requirements.

Again, the goal of the drug company is to create products it can sell. Drug companies are not scientific institutions, and they should not be thought of that way. This is not a criticism of them. This is merely a description of them. They were not established for the purpose of advancing science; they were established to sell products.

Many researchers see ethical problems with using children in clinical trials. What are the alternatives to ensure drugs are safe for children?

Research without consent is a very questionable undertaking. It's not always unethical. The difficult question is, Under what circumstances can we do research without the subject's consent? This is a question not just for young children. It's a question for anyone who might be made a nonconsenting subject, including people with certain kinds of mental illnesses and people with intellectual disabilities.

I think it is fair to say that the prevailing view among medical ethicists is that one can conduct research without the subject's consent if there is a good reason to believe that the research procedure itself will benefit the subject as well as provide information. When one is doing research that does not directly benefit the subjects and places them at some risk, conducting research without consent raises some very serious ethical problems.

For the most part, research on children is done under circumstances where, if the researcher's hypothesis is correct, the individual subject will benefit. For example, a child with otherwise untreatable cancer may be given chemotherapy in a research context because there is reason to believe, based on other research, that this new agent will improve the child's health.

So the general rule is that you don't start using a new drug on children. You use it first on adults and those who can consent. When it appears to work, you then move it into the child population, once you begin to understand the risks and benefits of that drug.

Removing Bias

What else needs to be done to improve the clinical trials process?

It has to be more open from beginning to end.

The review process needs to be open—and by "the review process" I mean the local review process, including institutional review boards that review this research. Institutional review boards are federally mandated review committees within research institutions. In order to use humans in research and to be able to submit the findings to the FDA, the company must submit the research protocols to institutional review committees for approval.

A review board must include at least one person from outside the institution. I don't think requiring only one institutionally nonaffiliated person is enough. It seems to me that the more the public knows, the better off we will be.

I think that we should try to remove as much bias as possible. There is really no question anymore that there is a relationship between who funds a study and chooses the investigators, and the study's outcome. When you compare the results of research paid for by private industry to research paid for by the NIH, you see very different results. This is troubling. I don't attribute this to corruption. I think the companies find researchers who are favorably inclined to their products and are willing to use the companies' protocols, which are designed in ways that will tend to yield positive results.

Let me give you an example: Many years ago, a drug company was working on an antibiotic for the treatment of otitis media, an ear infection in children. In trials, if the researchers used certain outcomes, such as hearing loss determined by one hearing test, it would appear that a particular antibiotic was better than another course of treatment. If the researchers used a different hearing test, it didn't appear that way.

So the question of who should select the outcomes to be used in a particular clinical trial becomes very important. Needless to say, it is in the interest of the drug company to

choose the outcome that is most likely to show positive results. We need to find a way to design trials so they are not
influenced by the profit goal.

Dr. Marcia Angell, in her recent book called *The Truth
About the Drug Companies*, which is pretty controversial, said
there should be a national institute that evaluates drugs. It is
not clear to me why the public should pay for research if the
result is a drug-company monopoly on products that would
be approvable due to this institute's research.

While drug companies should continue to pay for the research on their drugs, there's no reason why they should design the trials or pick the researchers. It would be best to have
a system where the drug companies say, We think this is a
good drug, and we're willing to spend $500 million finding
out if it is a good drug.

The companies would then provide that money to an independent agency that would choose the researchers and create the research design. I don't think that's realistic in the current political climate, but it's the kind of thing that needs to
be done. I think tinkering is not enough at this point.

Consumers Are Misinformed About Drugs

*How will improving clinical trials and making the data more
widely available increase drug safety?*

All drugs carry risks. Aspirin carries risks. You want people
to be well-informed users. And you don't want people to over-
estimate drugs' effectiveness. At this point, direct-to-consumer
drug advertising, the information drug companies now provide to consumers, is designed not to inform but to sell. A requirement that the raw data also be available to the public is
one way to try to counterbalance drug companies' positive
spin.

My guess is that if you asked people if Vioxx and Celebrex
are better than ibuprofen at treating the pain of arthritis, I
think most people would say yes. Do you agree?

I think most people would say yes.

But they would be wrong. The manufacturers don't make that claim, though you wouldn't know that by watching their ads, full of smiling, apparently pain-free people. The advantage of Vioxx and Celebrex and that class of drugs was supposed to be lower rates of side effects, in particular stomach bleeding.

There needs to be much better regulation of the tone of drug company ads, which certainly would seem to overstate the effectiveness of those drugs and understate the risks.

Consumers need better information. They need a better understanding of the limits of drugs and a better understanding of the risks.

"*Since these conflicts [of interest] can never be eradicated from professional life, their existence must be accepted and not equated with professional misconduct.*"

Most Drug Industry–Funded Research Is Not Biased

Ronald Bailey

In the following viewpoint, Ronald Bailey, book author and science correspondent for Reason Magazine, *counters claims that drug trials and researchers are influenced by their financial ties with pharmaceutical companies. He emphasizes that such conflicts of interest are not harmful. While he concedes that studies funded by the pharmaceutical industry are more likely to favor drugs than government-sponsored research, he attributes this to other factors besides bias. Tighter regulation of clinical research is unnecessary, Bailey insists, and collaboration between the medical community and drug companies should be encouraged because, in his assertion, it helps improve lives.*

Ronald Bailey, "Is Industry Funded Science Killing You?" *Reason*, vol. 39, no. 5, October 2007, pp. 34–43. Copyright © 2007 by Reason Foundation, 3415 S. Sepulveda Blvd., Suite 400, Los Ageles, CA 90034, www.reason.com. Reproduced by permission.

As you read, consider the following questions:

1. In Bailey's contention, what percentage of biomedical research funding is provided by the drug industry?

2. What theory does the author claim receives support from the 2006 *Journal of the American Medical Association (JAMA)* study that examined 202 cardiovascular drug trials?

3. Name six types of financial interests and conflicts that *JAMA* requires authors to disclose, according to Bailey.

In 2004 GlaxoSmithKline became the first major drug manufacturer to publicly disclose all the data from clinical studies of its products, including information that is usually treated as a trade secret. It was responding to a lawsuit by Eliot Spitzer, then New York's attorney general and now its governor [from January 2007 to March 2008], who accused Glaxo of hiding data about the safety and efficacy of one of its drugs. Sure enough, the company had concealed data indicating its antidepressant Paxil increased the risk of adolescent suicide. More-recent research suggests that link might not exist after all, but even if that proves true, it doesn't excuse the initial concealment.

A month later, Merck pulled its new pain reliever, Vioxx, off the market after clinical trial data showed that patients taking it had a 400 percent greater chance of heart attack than those taking the comparison drug, naproxen. Merck researchers implausibly argued that the difference was due not to damage caused by Vioxx but to the other drug's cardioprotective properties. No previous research had found that naproxen protects the heart.

For critics of the pharmaceutical industry, the Vioxx and Paxil incidents are evidence that conflicts of interest have thoroughly corrupted American medical research. "The Vioxx withdrawal serves as a reminder of the dangerous potential for conflict of interest that exists when pharmaceutical and other for-profit businesses control the dissemination of findings generated by medical research" warned a November 2004 editorial in the *Dayton Daily News*. In March 2005, the left-leaning Center for Science in the Public Interest (CSPI) pointed out that a Food and Drug Administration (FDA) panel that reviewed data on the risks posed by COX-2 painkillers like Vioxx included 10 researchers with financial ties to the companies that manufactured those drugs. Had the panelists with conflicts been excluded, a majority of the remaining members would have voted against approving Vioxx for distribution.

The Paxil incident prompted a June 2004 statement from the New York Attorney General's Office warning that "the ability of drug companies to pick and choose the research they provide doctors in support of their product is an outrageous conflict of interest and puts us all in harm's way." An August 2005 story about industry-funded medical research in the *San Jose Mercury News* quoted Sheldon Krimsky, a longtime critic of pharmaceutical companies, who asserted that "the entire system of drug testing is filled with conflicts of interest."

Typical or Rare?

There's no question that some companies have behaved badly in some cases. But are these cases typical or rare?

Activists, politicians, and other critics claim conflicts of interest are pervasive in pharmaceutical research. Several years ago CSPI established an Integrity in Science Project to investigate and publicize the destructive influence of industry-sponsored science. Not to be outdone, the Union of Concerned Scientists launched its own Scientific Integrity Program to "push for reforms that will protect our health, safety, and environment."

Politicians are jumping on the bandwagon, proposing more-stringent regulations of private clinical research. Sens.

Christopher Dodd (D-Conn.) and Edward Kennedy (D-Mass.) recently introduced the Fair Access to Clinical Trials Act, which would require all clinical trials to be registered in a central government database. Marcia Angell, a senior lecturer in social medicine at Harvard University, wants to ban privately funded clinical trials altogether. Instead, she proposes that drug companies be forced to pay into a government fund that would finance a new National Institute of Prescription Drug Trials to conduct all future clinical testing.

Supporters of such changes argue that conflicts of interest undermine public trust in and support for scientific research, endanger research subjects and patients, and boost medical costs by encouraging physicians and patients to use new treatments that are no better than cheaper alternatives. Yet public trust in biomedical research remains high, and that trust seems to be justified. Subjects in clinical trials hardly ever suffer serious harm, and instances in which dangerous side effects turn up after drugs are approved are relatively rare. Rather than making medicine unnecessarily expensive, pharmaceutical innovation ultimately reduces health care costs, because new drugs usually have advantages that pay off in lower medical bills.

The critics' concerns are not entirely groundless. Driven by self-interest, drug companies and researchers do occasionally hide data or run drug trials that produce data of scant clinical value. But private initiatives by medical journals, universities, and companies are already addressing these challenges, making government action unnecessary.

Unavoidable Conflicts

In 2005 *The Journal of the American Medical Association* reported that 5.6 percent of health spending in the U.S. goes to biomedical research, more than in any other country. In nominal dollars, funding for biomedical research in this country rose from $37 billion in 1994 to $94 billion in 2003. Even adjusted for inflation, that's an increase of almost 100 percent. The National Institutes of Health [NIH] provided 28 percent of that funding; industry gave 57 percent; state, local, foundation, and other federal agencies accounted for the remainder.

This cooperation between academia and industry has been essential to speeding new treatments from lab bench to hospital bedside. "By any measure, the interactions between academic research and industrial research and development, as epitomized by biotechnology, have been overwhelmingly positive," wrote Thomas Stossel, a professor of medicine at Harvard and a codirector of the Hematology Division at Boston's Brigham and Women's Hospital, in a 2005 *New England Journal of Medicine* article. "We should celebrate their achievements and protect the process that led to them."

But one man's beneficial cooperation is another's conflict of interest, a phrase that has acquired an inappropriately sinister connotation. As defined by the former Harvard epidemiologist Kenneth Rothman in a widely cited 1993 *New England Journal of Medicine* article, a conflict of interest is "any situation in which an individual with responsibility to others (which includes professional responsibilities) might be influenced, consciously or unconsciously, by financial and personal factors that involve self-interest."

Such conflicts are not at all unusual. David Korn, senior vice president for biomedical and health sciences research at the Association of American Medical Colleges, noted in 2000 that "conflicts of interest and commitment are ubiquitous in academic life (and indeed, in all professional life), and conflicting pressures inherent in the academic milieu, e.g., for faculty advancement, obtaining sponsored research funding, winning the acclaim of one's professional peers, competing for prestigious research prizes, and yes, desiring to alleviate human pain and suffering, all may be more powerful in influencing faculty behavior than the prospect of material enrichment." Such conflicts do not in themselves imply wrongdoing,

Concerns About Conflict of Interest Are Obsessive

Although initially focused on doctor-industry research relationships, concerns about conflict of interest have permeated every aspect of medicine and medical science. Only the imagination limits the extent of corruption now ascribed to financial conflict of interest. . . .

Corporate support of basic research, clinical research, CME [continuing medical education], clinical practice (through gifting and sampling by drug companies), practice guidelines, Food and Drug Administration (FDA) advisory committees, and drug formularies are all now examples of unacceptable financial conflicts of interest. Previously routine practices, such as the use of "ghostwriters" in the preparation of research or educational articles, or the matching of medical opinion leaders with medical audiences through "speaker's bureaus," have received special criticism.

Thomas P. Stossel,
Perspectives in Biology and Medicine, *Winter 2007.*

Korn stressed: "Since these conflicts can never be eradicated from professional life, their existence must be accepted and not equated with professional misconduct."

> The academic obsession with financial conflicts of interest not only endangers medical progress but also the very fundamentals that drive that progress. . . .

Corrupt or Well-Informed?

To illustrate the dangers allegedly posed by conflicts of interest, industry critics repeatedly point to a handful of atypical cases featuring erroneous results, suppressed data, or harmful side effects. In addition to such anecdotal evidence, they cite studies that show a correlation between industry funding and results that are favorable to the sponsors. As the researchers themselves acknowledge, however, there are benign explanations for such correlations.

In 1998 *The New England Journal of Medicine* published an article that claimed to show how commercial interests influenced the scientific evaluation of data on the relative safety and effectiveness of calcium-channel blockers, a class of drugs used to control high blood pressure. The study found that "authors who supported the use of calcium-channel antagonists were significantly more likely than neutral or critical authors to have financial relationships with manufacturers of calcium-channel antagonists (96 percent vs. 60 percent and 37 percent, respectively)." The authors concluded that this "strong association" meant the "medical profession needs to develop a more effective policy on conflict of interest."

But the study did not actually demonstrate that researchers had been inappropriately influenced by their ties to industry. The authors acknowledged as much, saying, "We believe that the authors we surveyed expressed their own opinions and were not influenced by financial relationships with pharmaceutical manufacturers." If financial relationships had no clearly discernible influence on the clinicians, what were the study's authors concerned about? Appearances. "We wonder how the public would interpret the debate over calcium-channel antagonists," the authors mused, "if it knew that most of the authors participating in the debate had undisclosed financial ties with pharmaceutical manufacturers."

Reviewing the data from that study, Thomas Stossel, the Harvard hematologist, noted that consultants working for companies that were not producing calcium-channel blockers were as likely to favor the drugs as those that consulted for companies that did produce them. Do scientists who do consulting work for one company have an interest in promoting its competitors' products? Stossel suggests a more logical explanation is that the researchers who consult with drug companies are better informed.

That argument seems credible, especially since, according to a 2002 meta-analysis of blood pressure treatments in the *Journal of the American College of Cardiology*, calcium-channel blockers have turned out to be at least as safe and effective as alternative drugs. Calcium-channel blockers are still widely used to control blood pressure. A 2005 study published in *The Lancet* found that a combination of calcium-channel blockers and angiotensin-converting enzyme (ACE) inhibitors was safer than a more conventional treatment combining diuretics with beta blockers. People with high blood pressure who take calcium-channel blockers are significantly less likely to develop diabetes than those treated with cheaper diuretics.

At the time of the 1998 *New England Journal of Medicine* article, activists claimed drug companies were duping physicians and patients into using more expensive treatments that were no more effective than earlier, cheaper medicines. Nine years later, further research shows the situation is more complicated: There is no one-size-fits-all treatment for hypertension. Based on what we know now, the more benign interpretation—that companies consulted with the most knowledgeable experts rather than that researchers favored companies that paid them—is more plausible.

Suspiciously Effective Medicine

A number of other studies have concluded that research results are biased by industry funding. Thirty-seven of those investigations were summed up in a review article by three Yale Medical School researchers that was published in *The Journal of the American Medical Association* (*JAMA*) in 2003. This meta-analysis found that "industry-sponsored studies were significantly more likely to reach conclusions that were favorable to the sponsor than were non-industry studies." But it also noted that "there are several possible reasons for this finding. It is possible that, given limited resources, industry only funds potentially winning therapies."

That explanation was bolstered by a 2006 study, also published in *JAMA*, that analyzed the outcomes of 202 randomized trials evaluating cardiovascular drugs reported between 2000 and 2005. Forty percent of the randomized drug trials funded by nonprofit organizations favored newer agents, compared to 54 percent of the jointly sponsored trials and 65 percent of the industry-funded trials.

The authors of the analysis suggested an explanation for these differences: "When the first trial report of a truly novel therapy is null or negative, it becomes less likely that any funding source will support subsequent studies. On the other hand, when the first trial of a truly novel therapy is positive, the likelihood of further trials is increased. These subsequent trials understandably and perhaps appropriately are more likely to be funded by for-profit organizations."

In other words, government and foundations are more likely to fund earlier stages of drug development, where the risk of failure is higher. Companies jump in to sponsor drug research at later stages of development, when success is more likely. Thus it is not surprising that industry-funded research is more likely to reach positive conclusions. If a drug company's trials regularly turned up negative findings, that would signal serious flaws in its drug discovery process.

Publication Bias Has Been Addressed

Another concern related to conflicts of interest is that publication bias dangerously skews the medical literature by favoring studies that reflect well on new therapies. "Studies with positive findings are more likely to be published than studies with negative or null results," said American Medical Association trustee Joseph M. Heyman at the organization's 2004 meeting. "We are concerned that this pattern of publication distorts the medical literature, affecting the validity and findings of systematic reviews, the decisions of funding agencies, and, ultimately, the best practice of medicine." Any tendency to put negative results into a file drawer and forget them can bias reviews of treatments reported in the medical literature, making them look more effective than they really are.

Because of the fear that industry funding and commercial motives skew research results, most prominent life science journals now require financial disclosures from researchers whose work they publish. *JAMA*'s disclosure policy is one of the more demanding, requiring authors to "provide detailed information about all relevant financial interests and relationships or financial conflicts within the past 5 years and for the foreseeable future (e.g., employment/affiliation, grants or funding, consultancies, honoraria, stock ownership or options, expert testimony, royalties, or patents filed, received, or pending), particularly those present at the time the research was conducted and through publication, as well as other financial interests (such as patent applications in preparation) that represent potential future financial gain." These disclosures, which must be included with each manuscript before it's submitted to peer reviewers, are typically published on the last page of the article. . . .

Collaboration Celebration

Collaboration between academia and industry should be encouraged, not attacked. In most areas of research, including computer science, geology, and chemistry, such ties are correctly seen as a source of innovation that has dramatically improved the quality of our lives during the last half-century. Given the potential life-or-death consequences for patients, collaboration between the pharmaceutical industry and medical researchers needs to be monitored, and adjustments should be made whenever abuses come to light. But through such private efforts as financial disclosure requirements, registration of clinical trials, and peer-reviewed publication of all clinical trial results, the scientific research enterprise has shown itself capable of protecting the validity of research results without new government regulations.

| *"It is a matter of moral concern that the trial process is not more transparent."*

Requiring Clinical Trials Registration Would Ensure Patients' Safety

Iain Chalmers, as told to the Bulletin of the World Health Organization

Sir Iain Chalmers, coauthor of Testing Treatments: Better Research for Better Healthcare, *is editor of the James Lind Library, an online resource on clinical trials. In the following viewpoint, he is interviewed by the* Bulletin of the World Health Organization *(WHO) about his support of a registry that would publicize all clinical research results. He advocates laws that require clinicians to register drug trials before they begin and to disclose their results when they end, to prevent researchers from hiding studies with negative outcomes. Such measures, he avows, would protect patients from pharmaceuticals shown to be dangerous during testing and would improve the efficiency of future trials.*

As you read, consider the following questions:

1. According to Chalmers, what problems exist for countries whose economies rely on the drug industry?

Iain Chalmers, as told to the *Bulletin of the World Health Organization*, "Raising the Standards of Clinical Trials and Research," vol. 85, no. 9, September 2007, pp. 658–659. Copyright © World Health Organization (WHO). Reproduced by permission.

2. What is the argument behind accepting China and India's registers in the WHO registry, as stated by Chalmers?

3. In the author's assertion, what question should be the yardstick by which clinical trials to be published are judged?

*B*ulletin of the World Health Organization (WHO): Why are clinical trials important, and how does the James Lind Library fit in?

Iain Chalmers: The James Lind Library is an educational resource helping people understand why trials are necessary. Public knowledge on how to assess whether claims about the effects of treatments are unacceptably dangerous or beneficial is not very available. What the James Lind Library attempts to do is explain that it is very easy to cause unintended harm with treatments and public health measures. The motivation for doing clinical trials is to try both to reduce the harm and increase the good that we do. But unless those trials are done carefully they may be misleading. It is important not just to acknowledge that conducting trials is important, but also that they should be done well, and analysed responsibly and validly. The James Lind Library's main responsibility is to introduce people to those principles.

Is the scientific, medical, clinical trial community adhering to these principles?

There are some areas where there has been improvement, such as in the design of studies and the quality of reports. But other problems have become more prominent, particularly the way in which investigators too frequently don't publish results of their studies when they are disappointed with them. Obviously that introduces a bias into what is available to the public and upon which they base treatments. Let's say you as a patient went to your doctor for treatment and your doctor only had access to studies showing positive effects of the treatment he or she offered to you, when in fact the important information on the negative effects had never been published. As a patient you would be receiving a treatment based on a decision distorted by not having access to all the relevant evidence. The treatment may not be effective and, even worse, it may be harmful.

Too Much Secrecy in Science

What can fix the system?

Governments can do much more, particularly their licensing authorities. Governments can set up measures through laws or regulations to insist that the whole clinical trial process is more transparent. That entails registering trials before their results are known. Within that registration process, which should be open to public scrutiny, the protocols for research should also be made public. One type of reporting bias is that whole studies don't get published. Another is that the outcomes that were initially envisaged as being important are not those that appear in the final report.

Governments can do various things to encourage transparency in clinical trials so that science and the discovery process can be more efficient. Too much secrecy exists in science, which makes it inefficient. Many analysts have shown that new drug discoveries during the last 20 years have been very disappointing considering the massive investment in research.

But a problem exists for any government when the pharmaceutical industry is a major part of that country's economy. Governments try to keep commercial operations happy; otherwise they face threats from companies to move their operations to other countries. There are forces operating against pushing for proper scientific behaviour. This is not a problem limited to people with vested commercial interests. It also exists throughout academia, where people do not systematically assess what is known already before embarking on new research.

The United States Takes Its First Step Toward Open Clinical Trials

On September 27, 2007, President [George W.] Bush signed into law the Food and Drug Administration Revitalization Act. . . .

[A] provision of the act requires sponsors of all clinically directive therapeutic trials to register their studies, at inception, in a public database sponsored by the National Library of Medicine. Although some aspects of this provision are not ideal, such as the delayed public availability of registration information on device trials and the noninclusion of phase I trials, mandatory registration represents a critical advance in making clinical trials of new treatments public knowledge. In this regard, the act is in accord with the position of the 12 general medical journals that form the International Committee of Medical Journal Editors, which have since 2005 required that trials be registered before they can be considered for publication, and the World Health Organization's International Clinical Trials Registry Platform.

Jeffrey M. Drazen, Stephen Morrissey, and Gregory D. Curfman,
New England Journal of Medicine, *October 25, 2007.*

How beneficial is the WHO International Clinical Trials Registry Platform [which works to make all clinical research transparent]?

This is a very important initiative, because there has been so little experience in developing trial registers. We are talking about experience that goes back only a decade and it is a great challenge to make sure it is done well. WHO, as the leading health organization in the world, has a leadership role to set standards. Quite rightly, WHO points out that greater transparency in clinical trials is a moral issue; and that it is a matter of moral concern that the trial process is not more transparent. After all, people are being invited to participate in clinical trials and it should be recognized that there is a duty of care to those people to ensure transparency.

All of WHO's activities depend on country support and it has the challenge of promoting progress at a rate that the major players can accept. It is obviously going to be a matter of judgement how best to do that. For example, a judgement was made recently that registers being developed in China and India should be accepted as primary registers in the WHO platform programme. The arguments in favour are that if you have two large economies like China and India signed up, as well as countries in Australasia, Europe and North America, you are encouraging recognition that this is a global issue that must be addressed at an international level. Others say it was premature to give such prominence to registers (in China and India) that are at very early stages of development.

Medical Journals Are Biased

How do you regard the International Committee of Medical Journal Editors' bid to make trialists and sponsors more accountable by agreeing not to publish results of any trial unless it has been publicly registered before the first patient's enrollment?

This was very important, but the trouble is that it came about two decades late. It was precipitated not by the strong scientific and moral reasons for trial registration, but by a law case brought by the attorney general of New York State against a drug company for withholding data that should have been in the public domain. It is a great shame that a law case was needed to make the world's leading medical scientific journals take a stand that they could have made years before.

Surveys have shown repeatedly that a great deal of rubbish is published in medical journals. We need to acknowledge more openly that the much-vaunted ritual of peer review leaves substantial room for improvement. One very senior editor, Richard Smith (a former editor of the *BMJ* [*British Medical Journal*]), has actually suggested in a recent article that journals should no longer be allowed to publish clinical trials because there are so many biases in the journal procedure itself. One of the ways in which medical journals make their money is by selling reprints of articles, and they know some studies are more likely than others to generate reprint income from commercial sponsors.

The most important thing is to ask the question: "Is the information that is being made available from clinical trial research the best that could be provided to promote the interests of patients and the public?" That should be the yardstick by which proposals are judged. Too often things get in the way—like academic credit, the profitability of journals or drug companies, or undeclared conflicts of interest among investigators. It is important to repeatedly remind oneself that the clinical trials business should be about trying to improve health care and the health of people. But as long as distortions exist in the research design and reporting processes, we won't have done as well as we could for the public interest.

Human Health Is at Stake

Can we ever expect full compliance and transparency from players involved in trials when so many interests are involved?

The Universal Declaration of Human Rights [adopted by the UN General Assembly in 1948] was a declaration of principles to which governments were invited to sign up. It is important that the declaration was issued because it provided benchmarks against which we think the behaviour of human beings to each other should be judged. More than any other actors in this arena, governments are responsible for trying to ensure those principles are observed. The same applies to the problems in current clinical trial enterprises. There are standards that should be set and everyone, particularly governments, should do what they can to ensure compliance.

But there will always be backsliding because the stakes are often very high, particularly the financial stakes for some players in this business. But something else is at stake too, and that is human health. It really does come down to a question on how you balance the interests of human beings who wish to improve and maintain their health, and what we can do about that, against other interests, such as financial, political and academic kudos.

"Registration of early exploratory trials . . . may slow development or even prevent innovation . . . without providing informational benefit to doctors."

Requiring Clinical Trials Registration Would Hinder Drug Development

International Federation of Pharmaceutical Manufacturers & Associations

In the following viewpoint, the International Federation of Pharmaceutical Manufacturers & Associations (IFPMA) asserts that the industry already publicizes certain clinical drug trial results and that requiring it to disclose all trial outcomes may backfire. While IFPMA agrees that researchers should disclose data from ongoing trials that may benefit patients and from some completed trials, it argues that mandatory reporting of early drug trials may retard drug development. Pharmaceutical companies may cease research if they must provide clinical trial information that may benefit their competitors, the federation warns.

International Federation of Pharmaceutical Manufacturers & Associations (IFPMA), "Pharmaceutical Industry Supports Move Towards Increased Clinical Trial Transparency to Help Doctors & Patients to Facilitate Informed Treatment Choices," May 18, 2006. www.ifpma.org. Copyright © 2005-2007 IFPMA. Reproduced by permission.

As you read, consider the following questions:

1. What is the Clinical Trials Portal, as the author describes it?

2. Why does IFPMA support timely publication of completed trials of approved medicines, in its own words?

3. According to IFPMA, to whom do drug companies already give full information on all clinical studies?

On the occasion of the International Clinical Trials Day Workshop, organized by the European Clinical Research Infrastructures Network (ECRIN) under the auspices of the European Commission and in collaboration with the WHO [World Health Organization], the IFPMA reaffirms its support for enhancing clinical trial transparency, to help provide doctors and patients with useful information.

IFPMA Director General Harvey E. Bale said: "Greater clinical trial transparency serves very important practical purposes. The pharmaceutical industry is committed to making clinical trial information available to facilitate informed treatment choices and participation in clinical studies. To this end, the IFPMA has invested heavily to facilitate public access to clinical trial information available on the Internet."

Clinical Trial Transparency

The first stage of the IFPMA Clinical Trials Portal was launched in September 2005. An improved portal, offering a user-friendly, multiple-criteria, advanced search function in English, French, German, Japanese and Spanish, was launched on 22 March 2006. The portal accesses registry information on more than 30,000 ongoing clinical trials and summary results of more than 5,000 completed trials of medicines approved for marketing in at least one country—and the numbers are growing daily.

Prof. Jacques Demotes, Coordinator of ECRIN and a clinical researcher in Bordeaux [France], commented: "I have

Mandatory Registration of Clinical Trials Interferes with the Drug Patent Process

Publication on a clinical trial register of the compound (intervention) name in combination with the indication (condition) can prevent valid patent protection being obtained. Each case will depend on its precise facts and the law of the country for which patent protection is sought. However, if relevant patent protection is not applied for before the registration of the trial the information will become part of the public domain information (prior art) against which the novelty and inventiveness of the patent application will be assessed. Under these circumstances, the information on the clinical trial register could prevent the grant of valid patent protection.

In theory, one way of avoiding this problem might be to apply for patent protection *before* information is published on the clinical trial register. However, in many countries, this is not possible as the patent application itself must contain data of the nature which the clinical trial is intended to generate. Countries with this requirement include Japan, Korea, China and Taiwan.

GlaxoSmithKline Government Affairs, Europe & Corporate,
"Disclosure of Clinical Trial Information,"
Global Public Policy Issues, June 2007. www.gsk.com.

found that the IFPMA Clinical Trials Portal offers a quick and easy way of finding information about ongoing trials, and helps me inform patients willing to participate in clinical trials."

The IFPMA has worked to realize the objective of increased clinical trials transparency through both policy and practical initiatives. In policy terms, the IFPMA supports public disclosure of information on ongoing clinical trials that are designed to generate useful therapeutic information for patients and other stakeholders. The IFPMA also requires timely publication by its member companies of results of completed trials of approved medicines, as these help further inform physician and patient decision making about appropriate treatments. The resulting public record also allows trials to be tracked to publication and facilitates wider patient and investigator participation.

Multiple Concerns with WHO's Proposal

The IFPMA welcomes the WHO's recent deliberations on recommendations for a global approach to clinical trial registration. Further dialogue between WHO, industry, regulators and other stakeholders is essential to develop sound policies for the benefit of patients. Industry suggests that flexibility must be incorporated in any final WHO recommendations, to help ensure registration of trials and to avoid inadvertently discouraging innovation. The IFPMA is very concerned that companies may refrain from conducting research and development in certain fields, if they feel they are obliged to provide competitors with sensitive information too early, or are unable to gain necessary legal protection for their innovations.

WHO is urging a standard that requires public registration of early exploratory trials. The potential implications of such a recommendation need to be considered carefully. This standard may slow development or even prevent innovation in certain cases, without providing informational benefit to doctors and patients. It is also important to acknowledge that full information on all clinical studies is always provided to regulatory authorities, ethics committees, investigators and patients who enroll in these studies. The IFPMA therefore urges that the WHO staff consult with regulatory agencies on the scope of trials to be registered, so that the benefits and risks can be assessed.

"The industry, represented at international level by the IF-PMA and at EU [European Union] level by the European Federation of Pharmaceutical Industries and Associations (EFPIA), has already done much to increase clinical trials transparency and stands ready to play a full and active part in discussions with the WHO and other stakeholders. The R&D [research and development] pharmaceutical industry is convinced that it is vital to arrive at a policy which encourages and promotes trial transparency, without discouraging the development of innovative new therapeutic approaches," noted Dr. Bale.

Periodical Bibliography

The following articles have been selected to supplement the diverse views presented in this chapter.

Emily Anthes and Scott Allen	"US Cancer Researchers Go Abroad for Trials," *Boston Globe*, December 29, 2007.
Roger Bate and Richard Tren	"Government-Controlled Pharmaceutical Research and Development: A Recipe for Disaster," *Health Policy Outlook*, May 22, 2006. www.aei.org.
Arthur Caplan	"Report Paints Grim Picture of Drug Trial Safety," *MSNBC*, September 28, 2007.
Sarah Colwell	"Bringing Drugs to Marketplace No Easy Task," *Colorado Springs Business Journal*, June 29, 2007.
Norman Fost and Robert J. Levine	"The Dysregulation of Human Subjects Research," *Journal of the American Medical Association*, November 14, 2007.
C.K. Gunsalus et al.	"Mission Creep in the IRB World," *Science*, June 9, 2006.
Gardiner Harris	"Report Assails F.D.A. Oversight of Clinical Trials," *New York Times*, September 28, 2007.
Ruth O'Halloran	"Transparency in Disclosure of Clinical Trial Information," *Journal of the European Medical Writers Association*, March 2006.
Pharmaceutical Research and Manufacturers of America	"Drug Discovery and Development: Understanding the R&D Process," February 2007. www.phrma.org.
Sarah Rubenstein	"When Drug Trials Go Wrong, Patients Have Little Recourse," *Wall Street Journal*, January 31, 2008.

OPPOSING
VIEWPOINTS®
SERIES

CHAPTER 2

Are Prescription Drugs Appropriately Regulated?

Chapter Preface

An estimated 21 percent (and by some estimates, 60 percent) of prescriptions are written for a purpose other than that for which the drug is approved by the Food and Drug Administration (FDA). Medications indicated to treat depression, for example, may be prescribed to patients with attention deficit disorders. Currently, according to the FDA's Center for Drug Evaluation and Research, "neither the FDA nor the Federal government regulate the practice of medicine. Any approved product may be used by a licensed practitioner for uses other than those stated in the product label." Called off-label prescribing or off-label use of drugs, the practice has benefited some patients and harmed or killed others. Now policy makers must carefully weigh the claims of those who clamor for more FDA oversight against those who eschew laws that might prevent doctors from offering new treatments to patients.

Those who maintain that off-label prescribing should be regulated are concerned for patient safety. Though the safety and effectiveness of a drug to treat psychosis, for example, has been established by clinical trials, its usefulness in relieving migraines has not. Maxwell J. Mehlman, director of the Law-Medicine Center at Case Western Reserve University, warns, "The fact that the product has been proven to be safe and efficacious for one use does not mean that it is safe and efficacious for any other." For instance, fen-phen, a combination of fenfluramine and phentermine, was commonly used off-label in the 1990s for the long-term management of obesity. Though the FDA had approved each drug when used alone for a short time, the combination over a longer term posed a serious heart risk in certain women, some of whom died. Critics of off-label prescribing also stress that doctors and patients need information on proper administration, dosage amounts, and warnings that do not come with drugs used for unapproved purposes. With these factors in mind, *Consumer Reports Best Buy Drugs* concludes,

> For every such example of positive off-label use, there are two or three that tell the other side of the story—of unsupported or potentially harmful off-label prescriptions. . . . Better information [provided by the FDA and others] to both doctors and consumers that will help them differentiate between good off-label use and bad off-label use. . . . would be highly valuable.

On the opposing side, though, are medical professionals who claim that drugs used off-label are cutting-edge treatments that simply have not been FDA-approved yet. James M. Beck and Elizabeth D. Azari, attorneys who have represented manufacturers in medical malpractice suits, assert, "The pace of medical discovery invariably runs far ahead of FDA's regulatory machinery, and off-label use is frequently 'state-of-the-art treatment.'" Off-label prescribing, in many physicians' views, may be the best way to treat illnesses that are less common, less researched, or more life-threatening than the ones for which the drugs are approved. They note that the unapproved use of drugs has saved the lives of cancer patients, just as the off-label use of thalidomide—officially intended as a sedative and hypnotic—has helped those with AIDS. Further, some people lament that requiring the FDA to regulate off-label prescriptions would interfere with the practice of medicine and impede doctors' efforts to provide the best possible care to patients.

Compounding the debate, in the spring of 2008 the FDA proposed new guidelines that would relax restrictions that pharmaceutical companies face when promoting off-label uses of their drugs. Strong opinions have been voiced about the thorny subject of drug regulation. The commentators featured in the following chapter scrutinize the FDA's efforts and discuss the effects of its regulations on drug accessibility and patient health.

| "No one who is familiar with the FDA culture and mind-set could possibly doubt that drug safety is paramount."

The FDA Actively Regulates Drug Safety

Henry I. Miller

Pharmaceuticals are rigorously regulated and their safety is continuously improving, argues Henry I. Miller in the following viewpoint. In his contention, current Food and Drug Administration (FDA) drug regulations are effective and appropriate, making more stringent regulations unnecessary. Tightening regulations, he predicts, would complicate the drug approval process, drive up prices, pull hugely beneficial drugs from the market, and hurt the patients they aim to protect. A doctor and former FDA official, Henry I. Miller authored The Frankenfood Myth: How Protest and Politics Threaten the Biotech Revolution.

As you read, consider the following questions:

1. What statistics does the author give to bolster his statement that drugs are getting better all the time?
2. What observation by Milton Friedman does Miller cite?

Henry I. Miller, "Strangling the Goose That Lays the Golden Drugs," *Regulation*, vol. 30, no. 2, Summer 2007, pp. 12–14. Copyright © 2007 Cato Institute. All rights reserved. Reproduced by permission.

3. According to the author, what are five reasons clinical trials may have what some consider "negative results"?

There is an old saying in Washington that when something has been repeated three times, it becomes a fact. The saying's most recent application is the supposed shortcomings in the safety of prescription drugs. The reality is that although all drugs have side effects—which can be serious and/or frequent—modern pharmaceuticals have wrought miracles in the control of pain, the treatment and prevention of infections, and the amelioration of diseases of aging such as arthritis and cancer.

Regulators need to balance patients' access to therapies with ensuring the safety of drugs. The consequences of poor decisions can be dire: promote access at the expense of safety, and a dangerous product can cause incalculable harm; overemphasize safety at the expense of access, and patients suffer from the absence of life-saving and life-enhancing medications.

Recently, beleaguered by congressional and other critics, the Food and Drug Administration [FDA] has been striving to demonstrate its commitment to drug safety—but it has done little to address a far more pervasive, more intransigent problem: unwise, unproductive, risk-averse regulation that itself has severe side effects. In spite of increasingly more powerful and precise technologies for drug discovery, purification, and production, during the past 20 years development costs have skyrocketed. The trends are ominous: the length of clinical testing for the average drug is increasing, fewer drugs are being approved, and the number of applications to the FDA by industry for marketing approval has been decreasing for more than a decade.

New Drugs Are Safe and Effective

In January [2007], the FDA announced new initiatives directed at the safety of new drugs, including a plan to perform a comprehensive assessment of the safety of some new drugs within 18 months of their introduction, and to issue a "report card" on their performance. Although this may sound plausible, it appears to be inconsistent with data showing that, in fact, newer drugs confer an advantage over older ones in reducing mortality. In a study of patients who took drugs during January–June 2000, those who took newer medications were less likely to die by the end of 2002. The estimated mortality rates were directly related to the time that had elapsed since approval of the drugs: for pre-1970 drugs, the estimated mortality rate was 4.4 percent, while the mortality rates for drugs approved during the 1970s, 1980s, and 1990s were 3.6 percent, 3.0 percent, and 2.5 percent, respectively. Not surprisingly, drugs are getting better all the time.

A related point is the myth, often cited as fact by regulators and members of Congress, that rapid advances in science are outstripping regulation. Although some fields, such as human gene therapy, offer significant challenges, innovations such as improved gene-splicing and separation and analytical technologies have led to the manufacture of more highly purified drugs—especially vaccines, hormones, and antibody preparations—that are less problematic for regulators.

The FDA's "cover" for these ill-advised innovations is that they are a response to a report on drug safety published last fall [2006] by the quasi-governmental Institute of Medicine [IOM]. However, the IOM's deeply flawed, one-sided analysis—bought and paid for the by the FDA, not coincidentally— will remedy few, if any, of the FDA's shortcomings. In fact, many of the recommendations would make the agency even more risk-averse, reduce further the number of drugs emerging from the research pipeline, and compromise public health.

Overregulation

Neither Congress nor the FDA (nor the IOM) is willing to admit that the agency's most significant problems are mismanagement and excessive risk-aversion. It is much easier to conclude that there is insufficient regulation and to throw more resources at the problem. (Recall economist Milton Friedman's wry observation that only government responds to a failed program by expanding it.) Meanwhile, regulators keep raising the bar for approval, especially for innovative, high-tech products. The FDA is requiring ever larger numbers of patients in clinical trials, its demands for post-marketing clinical trials have proliferated wildly, and "risk management" plans for newly approved drugs are punitive and have been inconsistently applied.

Historically, the pendulum has swung back and forth about what kinds of problems predominate in the regulation of drug development. Thirty years ago, the concerns were primarily about "drug lag"—indolent reviews and approvals by the FDA that put Americans at a disadvantage to consumers in other countries. But in recent years, there have been repeated accusations about what might be called "drug leap"—a supposedly "too cozy" relationship between regulators and industry, and too little attention paid to drug safety, possibly as the result of regulators' struggling to meet arbitrary deadlines. No longer are federal regulators called to account for the unnecessary deaths of patients who do not get the new drugs they need in a timely way.

The FDA's recent attempts to convince its critics that it takes drug safety seriously have been unnecessary, unseemly, and unsuccessful. No one who is familiar with the FDA culture and mind-set could possibly doubt that drug safety is paramount—if for no other reason than because approving a product that proves to be dangerous can ruin a government career.

The FDA has once again become a reed in the political winds, fanned by many influential leaders of Congress. Given the pro-regulatory leanings of many of the new committee chairmen, including Sen. Ted Kennedy (D-Mass.), Rep. John

Dingell (D-Mich.), and Rep. Henry Waxman (D-Calif.), hearings and new lawmaking will focus on alleged under-regulation and the need for additional power and resources for the FDA. The agency will be encouraged to regulate more aggressively and punitively, and will be only too happy to comply. User-fees on drug companies—another name for a discriminatory tax on a single industrial sector—will likely be increased.

Unnecessary Measures

Two bills—undoubtedly the harbinger of things to come—were introduced in the Senate in February [2007].[1] Senators Kennedy and Michael Enzi (R-Wyo.), the chairman and ranking Republican, respectively, of the Health, Education, Labor, and Pensions Committee, proposed legislation that would grant the FDA new authority to impose safety requirements on medicines after they have been approved for marketing. The legislation would also require registration of clinical trials and the reporting of their results in public databases. In addition, Sen. Chris Dodd (D-Conn.) and Sen. Charles Grassley (R-Iowa) introduced legislation that would create within the FDA a center to oversee the safety of drugs after they go on the market.

These bills are the culmination of years of drug company-bashing by a small number of activists and members of Congress who have seized on high-profile events such as deficiencies in the labeling of antidepressants and the discovery of previously unknown side effects of various widely used drugs. They will discourage drug development by making it more difficult and expensive, at a time when an aging American population desperately needs new and improved (and cheaper) medicines, and when pharmaceutical research is already ailing.

The FDA is already the nation's most powerful and omnipresent regulator. The Kennedy-Enzi bill would grant it new

1. At press time, Congress had not debated or voted on either bill.

An FDA Official Details the Rigorous Drug-Monitoring Process

We have on our staff at the FDA approximately 50 safety evaluators and epidemiologists, who, on a daily basis, review the adverse events that we received on the prior day, particularly those that are of a serious nature. We follow up certain kinds of adverse events in great detail.

We receive approximately 1,000 reports every day at the FDA. Those are entered immediately into our adverse event reporting system. Then they are triaged to the safety evaluators electronically. Those events pop up on their computer screen. They review those events, look for those that are serious or important, and make a decision as to whether they need to request further information on those cases, having reviewed the narrative of that particular case. Each safety evaluator is assigned a certain series of drugs in their domain. . . .

Our safety evaluators are trained pharmacists, usually with advanced degrees in pharmacy. They tend to focus on a limited number of drugs. They're constantly looking at the reports that they're receiving and comparing them with reports that they've received in the past days, weeks, months, or years, to determine whether or not there's a pattern that merits their further or closer attention.

Our safety evaluators also will often follow up directly with the reporter of a particular case to get more information, to assess whether or not the adverse event that's reported is related to the drug in question.

PBS Frontline, interview with Paul Seligman, Dangerous Prescription, November 4, 2002. www.pbs.org.

authority, supposedly to ensure the safety of drugs, and would require drug approvals to be accompanied by post-marketing risk evaluation and mitigation strategies (REMS) that are intended to help firms and regulators assess post-marketing adverse-event reports and communicate risk information to the public. REMS could include mandatory post-marketing safety studies, restrictions on which providers can prescribe or dispense a drug, and limitations on direct-to-consumer advertising.

But the FDA already has the authority to require REMS as well as detailed Risk Management Actions Plans (RiskMAPs) when regulators feel that they are necessary. It is revealing that RiskMAPs have been overused and abused: at times the exhaustive (and exhausting) list of requirements for physicians, pharmacists, and patients seems more appropriate for weapons-grade plutonium than a pharmaceutical. Some Risk-MAPs have contained requirements such as mandatory enrollment in patient registries, limited distribution, and prescribed patient behavior (such as the use of two kinds of contraception, in the case of one drug).

Claims That Drug Companies Cherry-Pick Clinical Studies Are Exaggerated

The requirement that drug companies disclose advanced clinical trials in a public database is based on concerns that "negative" results are often obscured or simply not reported. It is intended to prevent companies from "cherry-picking" studies, divulging only those that yield favorable results and suppressing the rest. Those concerns are exaggerated. Nothing in our society is currently more stringently regulated and monitored than drug development. During each phase of clinical testing, the FDA reviews and must grant permission for every clinical trial, and has access to all of the proprietary information about the drug. When the manufacturer has accumulated evidence that the drug is safe and effective, as part of the application for marketing approval, the results of every trial and everything else that is known about the drug (both in the United States and abroad) must be reported to the FDA. Statistical analysis must be performed in an appropriate and pre-specified manner. Moreover, the FDA serves as a repository for data on similar drugs made by other manufacturers. All of this prevents statistical "cherry-picking" or "data mining" that could mislead regulators.

Clinical trials databases are useful to individual patients who want to know if they are eligible for a clinical trial that is under way—a function already served by www.clinicaltrials-.gov. But, except for offering a bonanza to plaintiffs' attorneys trolling for business, the benefits of a publicly available database of clinical trial results are dubious.

There is also the question of the meaning of "negative results" in clinical trials. In the context of scientific and clinical experiments, the term has a meaning very different from the common usage. Such trials are seldom "negative" in the sense of revealing that the drug being tested inflicts harm; rather, the term typically connotes that the tested drug may not be useful or applicable to the indications (uses) for which approval is being sought. The reasons can include: insufficient statistical power (that is, number of patients) in the study; inappropriate choice of route, dose or frequency of administration, or in the stratification of subjects; or simply a failure of the drug to be effective for the indication for which it was tried.

Jokes and Laws

The Dodd-Grassley proposal is even worse. It would create within the FDA an anti-drug entity with strong incentives to argue for the non-approval or market withdrawal of drugs that have significant side effects even if they offer huge net benefits. (We have seen this already from certain factions within the agency.)

These proposed legislative remedies for the FDA's problems, with more planned for later in the year in both the House and Senate, are analogous to the discredited medical practice of bleeding the patient with leeches. By intensifying the FDA's notorious risk aversion, the new measures will inflate even further the costs, difficulty, and uncertainty of drug development and reduce the number of drug candidates that begin and complete clinical testing. They will drain the life's blood from innovation and inflict harm on patients. If these pieces of legislation are enacted, they will validate yet again [cowboy entertainer] Will Rogers's quip about Congress: "Every time they make a joke, it's a law. And every time they make a law, it's a joke." As usual, the joke will be on us.

> *"Patients who are terminally ill . . . have a fundamental right to decide . . . whether to take the risks associated with . . . investigational drugs."*

Terminal Patients Should Be Allowed to Take Unapproved Medications

Scott Ballenger, as told to Margot Adler

Attorney Scott Ballenger brought a lawsuit against the Food and Drug Administration (FDA) in which he and his client, the Abigail Alliance, maintained that dying patients have a right to try experimental drugs. The following viewpoint is excerpted from his discussion of the case on National Public Radio's Justice Talking *with host Margot Adler. Ballenger reasons that since the FDA considers investigational drugs safe enough to test on humans in clinical trials, it should grant people unable to participate in trials access to those medicines as well. Patients with no treatment alternatives, he argues, should be able to weigh the risks and decide for themselves without interference from the FDA.*

Scott Ballenger, as told to Margot Adler, "Should Dying Patients Have a Right to Use Experimental Drugs?," *Justice Talking* on National Public Radio, April 16, 2007. Reproduced by permission.

As you read, consider the following questions:

1. For what reasons might patients be denied entry into clinical trials, according to Ballenger?
2. In Ballenger's opinion, how does the *Abigail* case differ from the case that dealt with the drug Laetrile?
3. What conclusion does Ballenger draw from the *Cruzan* case?

M*argot Adler: Tell us about the case you argued*, Abigail Alliance vs. von Eschenbach.

Scott Ballenger: Well, it's a fundamental rights, constitutional privacy case in the same tradition as the contraception cases and a series of fundamental rights cases the court has decided for the last 100 years, really. Our claim is that patients who are terminally ill and have exhausted all of the approved treatment options have a fundamental right to decide for themselves whether to take the risks associated with treatment with investigational drugs. And we're talking here about drugs that the FDA itself has cleared for substantial human testing, drugs that are currently in phase II human clinical trials. And my clients are patients who for one reason or another have tried to get into the trials but simply can't, usually just because the trials are frequently too small to accommodate all of the people who desperately need access to the drug, or because sometimes the trials come with restrictive criteria for eligibility, like that you can't have been treated aggressively with some other drug in the past.

As I understand it, most privacy law is really a negative, the right to be free from, for example, invasive treatment at the end of life. So I've never heard that privacy really works as far as the right to gain something new.

Well, this is actually a negative right exactly like all of the others you're talking about. No one is claiming a right to affirmative government assistance of any kind. All that we're ask-

Cancer Patients Should Be Permitted to Try Provenge and Other Experimental Vaccines

The trial [for Provenge prostate cancer vaccine] did show a benefit with an average four-and-a-half month improvement in patient longevity over the placebo group. For the men who received Provenge there was a 41% overall reduction in the risk of death. This improvement occurred even though over 50% of the patients tested were expected to die within 36 months of starting the trial.

It is well known from the Provenge trial as well as from trials of other cancer vaccines that the patients receiving the vaccines tend to live longer and that they respond better to subsequent treatments. Researchers believe that increased longevity is the best measure of a vaccine therapy result. . . .

The FDA has called for further testing which will delay the approval of Provenge for at least two years. Many prostate cancer patients will die before approval is granted.

Charles A. Reinwald,
speech at Right-to-Live Day Rally, Rockville, MD,
September 18, 2007. www.cancercurecoalition.org.

ing is that the FDA get out of my clients' way and allow them to use their own private resources to fight for their own lives in life-threatening circumstances.

Patients with No Treatment Alternatives

There was a case in 1979 over the drug Laetrile, which some patients believed was a cure for cancer, but which hadn't been approved by the FDA. Patients sued and lost in the Supreme Court. Why is your case any different?

Well, the fundamental difference between the *Rutherford* case and Laetrile and what we're asking for is the patients in the *Rutherford* case were asking to take something that had not been tested at all, had not been approved by the FDA for human clinical testing at all. And they were proposing to forego conventional therapy in order to do it. And in that context the Supreme Court said that there is, even for terminally ill patients, there is an important relationship between the efficacy of a drug and its safety, because if you are foregoing proven conventional treatment in order to take something that is untested and unproven then doing that may affirmatively harm you in the sense that you forego treatment that might help you. We are in this lawsuit talking only about people who have exhausted all of the approved treatment alternatives, so there's nothing in the way of conventional therapy that they're passing up. And we're only talking about drugs that, unlike Laetrile, the FDA itself concedes are safe and promising enough to be tested in substantial numbers of human beings. Phase II trials usually involve somewhere between 200 and 1,000 people, and the FDA recognizes in the case of these drugs that there is enough evidence of safety and enough evidence of potential efficacy for those trials to be ethical. All that we're saying is that the FDA should give the same freedom to patients who are unable to gain a spot in the trial, that it is simultaneously given to the patients who aren't lucky enough to win those few coveted spots in the clinical trial.

Where does your case stand now?

Well, the D.C. Circuit Court of Appeals ruled for us in a three-judge panel. The way that federal court of appeals cases are usually decided is that the case is assigned to a three-judge panel of judges. The D.C. Circuit Court of Appeals as a whole, though, is 10 judges, and they have granted re-hearing "in bank," which means a re-hearing in front of the full panel of 10. So we had a couple of weeks ago re-argument of the case in front of the full panel of 10 judges and they will re-decide the case sometime this spring.[1]

And what has the main argument by the FDA been?

Well, the FDA's main argument is that their policies in this area should be subjected to nothing other than basic rationality scrutiny.

What does that mean?

Well, the basic divide in constitutional law is that if a government policy implicates fundamental rights it has to be narrowly tailored to a compelling state interest. If it doesn't implicate fundamental rights then it only has to be rational. And the FDA's position in the case has been that no fundamental rights are implicated in this context and therefore all they have to show is basic rationality.

Protecting the Progress of Science?

And if the ruling is upheld, what are the implications for the FDA?

Well, it's hard to say exactly. In a very real sense, all that this case has been about thus far has been standard of review, what level of justification the FDA has to provide to defend its policies. If we win in the D.C. Circuit, then the case will go back to the district court under the narrowly tailored or compelling state interests standard, and the FDA will be forced to provide truly compelling justifications for interfering with patient freedom in this area. It is possible that the FDA could articulate truly compelling justifications for interfering with patient rights and if so then they would prevail. All that will happen as the result of a victory by Abigail Alliance in this case is a return to the district court and an opportunity for the FDA to explain why what it's doing is genuinely justified by compelling state interest.

And I would imagine that they will argue that scientific testing would be imperiled and so forth?

1. The court determined in August 2007 that dying patients do not have a constitutional right to try drugs that have not been FDA-approved.

They will. Absolutely. And to some extent those arguments will be persuasive. But the Abigail Alliance's fundamental point in this lawsuit is that there may be circumstances in which it is necessary to restrict access to experimental drugs in order to protect the progress of science, but it is not necessary to restrict access to experimental drugs for everyone in order to protect the progress of science. For instance, if your concern is about incentives to participate in clinical trials, it makes no sense to deny the drugs to patients who are ineligible for the trial.

Do you see this as a case that could easily wend its way up to the Supreme Court?

I do. I believe it is the next great civil liberties case and that the court should take it.[2]

I've heard that in arguing your case that you've compared it to some degree to the Cruzan *case, which talked about being able to refuse treatment at the end of life. Tell me a little bit about this argument.*

In the *Cruzan* case the Supreme Court recognized that any patient, even an actually relatively healthy patient, has a fundamental constitutional right to refuse all medical treatment—including proven medical treatment that could save their lives—and die. Well, if people have a fundamental right to refuse all medical treatment and die, then why in the world don't they have a fundamental right to take a course of medical treatment that the FDA thinks is simply unproven and that might kill them? It doesn't make any sense to say that the federal Constitution protects a right to choose to die but not a right to choose to fight for your life.

2. In January 2008, the Supreme Court declined to hear the case.

| "The vast majority of drugs in phase I trials are not lifesaving; they are not even life-prolonging."

Terminal Patients Should Not Be Allowed Access to Unapproved Medications

Ralph W. Moss

According to Ralph W. Moss in the following viewpoint, terminally ill patients do not have a right to take drugs that have not completed clinical trials. When medications are still being tested, he points out, scientists know very little about them and their benefit is often overestimated. Allowing patients to try such treatments, he avows, would endanger their lives, undermine the Food and Drug Administration's (FDA) efforts to evaluate drug safety and effectiveness, and negatively impact the clinical trial process. Moss, a cancer consultant, has written eleven books and hundreds of reports on cancer treatments.

As you read, consider the following questions:

1. How did the FDA oppose the Abigail Alliance's efforts to reduce drug testing requirements, according to Moss?

Ralph W. Moss, "No Way to Save a Life: Allowing Terminally Ill Cancer Patients Access to Drugs That Have Not Completed Clinical Trials Is a Dangerous Move," *New Scientist*, vol. 190, June 3, 2006, p. 21. Copyright © 2006 Reed Elsevier Business Publishing, Ltd. Reproduced by permission.

2. How does the author respond to claims that FDA regulations interfere with efforts that could save lives?

3. According to Moss, how would expanded access to experimental drugs affect clinical trial enrollment?

Last month [May 2006], the US Court of Appeals for the District of Columbia made a decision of huge consequence. It ruled [in *Abigail Alliance v. von Eschenbach*] that terminally ill cancer patients have a constitutional right to treatments that have not yet been approved by the Food and Drug Administration (FDA). As long as such drugs have completed phase I clinical trials, the court stated, they should be made available to any patient who requests them.

The three-judge panel split 2-1 in favour of a suit brought by the Abigail Alliance for Better Access to Developmental Drugs, a patient advocacy group that has been lobbying hard to bring new medicines to terminally ill patients. The decision is ominous because it is likely to undermine the drug evaluation process, which has been under attack for over a decade. In another worrying development, last November [2005] Republican senator Sam Brownback introduced a bill into the Senate aimed at accelerating the approval system for drugs, biological products and medical devices. It would give patients access to treatments that have shown promise but have not been proven. If enacted, this bill could lead to an anarchic jumble of ineffective and potentially unsafe treatments on the market.

Accelerated Drug Approvals

The *Abigail* case and the congressional initiative are part of a widespread effort to reduce the requirement that new drugs go through extensive and rigorous testing before being sold to the public. The FDA, and the Bush administration that it serves, have ostensibly opposed Abigail's efforts. For example, the FDA argued that it already had plans to make potentially

The Abigail Alliance's Push for Access to Unapproved Drugs Puts Physicians in an Awkward Position

The essence of the [Abigail] Alliance's clinical argument is that terminally ill patients should have the choice of using experimental drugs in consultation with physicians. "All [the plaintiffs] ask is that the government get out of their way, so that they can use their own private resources to fight for their own lives at the inherently uncertain frontiers of modern science," [reads the Alliance's initial brief.] Consistent with current market theory, the [Court of Appeals] panel's opinion [supporting access to unapproved drugs] shifted the risks to the patient but also to the physician.

Physicians already face considerable pressure from patients who demand medications that are heavily marketed through direct-to-consumer advertising. As contentious as such advertising has been, allowing access to unapproved pharmaceuticals places physicians in the uncomfortable position of prescribing drugs with unknown risk profiles that may be more harmful than beneficial, explaining to patients why simply calling something lifesaving does not make it so, or being candid that medicine has nothing more to offer. While this is precisely the risk-benefit discussion that physicians should be having with patients, there is a substantial added burden when discussing drugs that have not completed appropriate clinical trials, especially when no data or published reports exist to support the physician's professional opinion of safety and efficacy. As the government argued to the panel, terminally ill patients are particularly vulnerable to promises that unproven treatments will be effective.

Peter D. Jacobson and Wendy E. Parmet,
Journal of the American Medical Association, *January 10, 2007.*

lifesaving drugs available before the completion of the lengthy three-phase clinical trial process. It also claimed that allowing large numbers of patients to receive unapproved drugs could put many of them at unacceptable risk, even if they were terminally ill. But the FDA's opposition was undercut by its own increasing reliance on the so-called accelerated approval programme, under which drugs are often approved before there is proof of clinical benefit.

One drug approved in this way was Iressa, a treatment for advanced lung cancer, which was given the green light by the FDA on the basis of questionable phase II trial results, ignoring compelling phase III trials showing that the drug was ineffective and more toxic than anticipated. So the drug approval process had already begun to fray at the edges before the Appeals court judges made their ruling last month. Their decision could accelerate that trend: the judges ruled that the FDA's normal regulatory activity interfered with efforts that could save a terminally ill patient's life.

While that sentiment is seemingly humane, it is based on a false premise, for it wildly overestimates the effectiveness of most new anti-cancer drugs. It ignores the fact that there are very few truly lifesaving drugs for the advanced stages of any kind of adult cancer. Most new "targeted" drugs, when combined with conventional chemotherapy, extend life by a few months at best. Yet these drugs are widely perceived as a revolutionary new departure in cancer treatment—an impression that drug companies have done little to dispel.

The Importance of Phase II and III Clinical Trials

The vast majority of drugs in phase I trials are not lifesaving; they are not even life-prolonging. More crucially, it is only through the successful completion of arduous phase II and phase III trials that drugs can ever be proven to be beneficial. By allowing the drug approval process to be truncated, as the judges propose, the potential for gathering important information on the safety, toxicity and effectiveness of new treatments is severely curtailed. This spells doom for the randomised clinical trial process. Few patients are likely to agree to enter phase II or III trials with the same agent that will be freely available after small phase I studies. Most likely, cancer patients will increasingly fall prey to exaggerated claims for various half-baked drugs, as a result of skilful manipulation of public opinion through publicity.

At the end of phase I trials, scientists, industry officials, regulators and the public still know next to nothing about the drug in question, least of all its effectiveness. The purpose of phase I is simply to evaluate a drug's safety, determine a workable dosage range and identify side effects. Granted, some clinical effects such as tumour shrinkages may be seen in a few patients, but this is incidental information—and the temporary shrinkage of a tumour seldom correlates with a prolongation of life.

Much of the information that patients receive about new drugs is of a dubious kind. The FDA, for all its shortcomings, is the main barrier that exists against the domination of the market by hype. But since the Clinton years, and especially during the George [W.] Bush era, the FDA's vigilance over the cancer drug marketplace has been steadily eroded. The repercussions of this latest judicial decision are potentially disastrous. If it is allowed to stand,[1] it will make the task of determining which drugs actually work much more difficult. That is hardly in the interest of cancer patients.

1. The decision was reversed by an appeals court in August 2007, and the Supreme Court later refused to hear the case. The original decision, that terminally ill patients do not have a constitutional right to unapproved drugs, still stands.

> "BTC drugs will not improve patient access to medications. The lack of access to drugs is tied to our fragmented, poorly-coordinated and costly health care system."

The FDA Should Not Allow Pharmacists to Dispense Behind-the-Counter Drugs

Rick Kellerman

Rick Kellerman is board chair of the American Academy of Family Physicians (AAFP), a national medical organization that promotes the specialty of family medicine. The following viewpoint is excerpted from a letter he wrote to the Food and Drug Administration (FDA) on behalf of the academy. In it, he laments that proposals to make certain drugs accessible through pharmacists rather than doctors are a poor solution to problems in our health care system. Patients who take drugs need to be monitored by physicians, he stresses, and pharmacists are not trained to perform that role, in his opinion.

Rick Kellerman, "Letter from the American Academy of Family Physicians to Andrew C. von Eschenbach of the Food and Drug Administration," *American Academy of Family Physicians*, November 28, 2007. Copyright © 2007 American Academy of Family Physicians. Reproduced by permission.

As you read, consider the following questions:

1. According to the author, what does patient compliance with drugs involve?

2. What is Kellerman's concern regarding patients with multiple chronic conditions?

3. By focusing on the role of the pharmacist, the plan to create BTC drugs ignores what, in the author's opinion?

D ear Dr. von Eschenbach:

On behalf of the 93,800 members of the American Academy of Family Physicians (AAFP), I am writing in response to your proposal about the public health benefit of permitting some prescription drugs to be behind-the-counter (BTC) with the requirement that they be dispensed by a pharmacist but without consultation with a physician. The Academy strongly opposes this proposal. Following are our reasons for our opposition.

A Narrow Focus Ignores the Broader Problem

The information in support of this proposal contained in the *Federal Register* is incomplete. The background materials posit a potential increase in patient access to drugs; describe the use of a BTC class in many Western countries (if drugs are "suitable for self-medication, including self-diagnosis, with the intervention of a pharmacist and low potential for side effects"); and emphasize the training and knowledge of pharmacists.

Unfortunately, the background information is focused narrowly on the purported goal of allowing patients simpler access to drugs via pharmacists and does not include a broader perspective on the effect this proposal would have on the already fragmented American health system and patient care. Specifically, the crucial role that physicians play in diagnosis and prescribing drugs to their patients is not mentioned and more broadly, whether or not BTC drugs are a logical step toward the goal of an integrated, coordinated system of quality patient care. Our question is what problem this proposal is trying to solve and is this plan the best way to solve it? In our view, this plan is yet another symptom of a dysfunctional health care system, i.e., the perceived inability of patients to get medications, and should be addressed by overarching reform. With that perspective in mind, following are our responses to questions posed by FDA that are relevant to physicians.

Pharmacists Cannot and Should Not Do the Jobs of Physicians

What might the impact of BTC be on patient access?

We believe that BTC drugs will not improve patient access to medications. The lack of access to drugs is tied to our fragmented, poorly-coordinated and costly health care system. Access will be improved with a patient-centered medical home directed by a primary care physician (see further description below), and an appropriate history, examination and diagnosis performed by a physician. In addition, access will be improved if we can achieve health care coverage for all.

What might the impact of BTC be on patient compliance with drug therapy?

Compliance with drug therapy will not be improved with a new class of BTC drugs. Patient compliance with drugs involves a complex mix of an understanding of one's disease, appropriate follow-up with the diagnosing physician and ongoing monitoring by the physician of the appropriate medication(s) for side effects or reduced efficacy.

Please comment on the following criteria for what roles a pharmacist or other health professional might play, which are included below for discussion purposes. For example, a pharmacist or other practitioner licensed by law to dispense prescription drugs prior to sale might (A) Review or conduct an initial screen-

A Comprehensive Review Finds Few Benefits of Behind-the-Counter Drugs

Little evidence supports the establishment of a pharmacy or pharmacist class of drugs in the United States at this time, as either a fixed or a transition class. The evidence that is available tends to undermine the contention that major benefits are being obtained in the countries that have such a class. This conclusion is substantiated by six points. (1) Reliable and valid studies that examine the effect of different drug distribution systems on overall health and health care system costs do not exist. (2) While a pharmacy or pharmacist class exists in all 10 countries, it is not used with any frequency in any of them to facilitate the movement of drugs to sale outside specialized drug outlets. (3) The European Union has decided not to impose any particular drug distribution system on its member countries because it has found no evidence of the superiority of one system over another. (4) There is no clear pattern of increased or decreased access to drugs as nonprescription products where a pharmacist or pharmacy class exists. (5) While a pharmacy or pharmacist class is assumed by some to improve safeguards against drug misuse and abuse, in the 10 countries these safeguards are easily circumvented, and studies show that pharmacist counseling is infrequent and incomplete. (6) Experience in Florida with a class of drugs similar to a pharmacist class has not been successful; pharmacists have not regularly prescribed these drugs, and recordkeeping requirements have not been followed.

U.S. General Accounting Office,
Prescription Drugs: Value of a Pharmacist-Controlled
Class Has Yet To Be Demonstrated, *August 1995.*

ing for clinical laboratory test results, contraindications, or drug interactions; (B) Counsel the patient on safe use; (C) Monitor for continued or safe or effective use.

We agree that pharmacists are trained to be experts on drugs and drug interactions. We strongly oppose pharmacists performing the remainder of the suggested roles. These activities are the purview of the physician and not of the pharmacist. Further, the examples do not take into account patients with multiple chronic conditions who may take numerous medications and need a physician to treat them as a "whole person" and not by individual disease state. Finally, in the event of a serious drug interaction, patients should call their primary care physician and not a pharmacist.

Should reimbursement be available to pharmacists for providing services associated with BTC dispensing? What type? What type of billing procedures could be utilized and how would third party companies facilitate such reimbursement?

The AAFP is strongly opposed to reimbursement for pharmacists for providing BTC drugs. Currently, physicians are not paid appropriately for prescribing medications done in the context of diagnosis and treatment. Payment for dispensing of BTC drugs by individuals lacking physician knowledge and training would be an inappropriate use of scarce medical dollars.

Pharmacists Should Be Part of, Not Separate from, the Health Care Team

In general, what are the benefits and costs to the health care system as a whole related to BTC availability?

As stated in our introductory paragraph, the Academy believes that a new class of BTC is under discussion due to overarching problems in the entire American health care system. We believe that the entire system should be transformed so that issues such as access to the appropriate medications are handled within a broader framework, i.e., the patient-centered medical home. Following is information on this concept.

The patient-centered medical home is a proven model in health care delivery that the AAFP has proposed along with the American College of Physicians, the American Academy of Pediatrics and the American Osteopathic Association. In this new model, the traditional doctor's office is transformed into the central point for Americans to organize and coordinate their health care, including prescription drugs, based on their needs and priorities.

At its core, the patient-centered medical home model is an ongoing partnership between each person and a primary care physician. This new model provides improved access through e-mail communication and same-day appointments and secure online tools to help consumers manage their health information, review the latest medical findings and make informed decisions. Patients receive reminders about necessary appointments and screenings, as well as other support to help them and their families manage chronic conditions such as diabetes or heart disease, including the use of prescription medications.

The primary care physician's practice that serves as a medical home includes a team of specialists and other health care providers such as nutritionists and physical trainers. The primary care physician makes sure that the team works together to meet all of the patient's needs in an integrated, "whole person" fashion. In our view, pharmacists would be incorporated into a team of providers who would be responsible for a patient's care. The FDA's proposal to detach pharmacists from this team and allow them to deliver drugs independently would be a step away from this goal.

The patient-centered medical home will be recognized by an independent organization so that payers can be assured that their investment in this model of care delivery will result in a higher standard of care.

We understand the FDA's concern about increasing access to medications, particularly to those who are uninsured. The solution proposed does not address the complexities involved in today's pharmaceutical world. More importantly, with its narrow focus on the role of the pharmacist, the plan ignores the larger health care system, and, in particular, the crucial role that is played by a physician whose goal is to coordinate patient care.

> *"There is another factor to consider: Who stands to benefit from the latest alarm about an apparent upturn in youth suicide rates?"*

The FDA's Black Box Warnings on Antidepressants Did Not Cause an Increase in Youth Suicides

Alison Bass

The Food and Drug Administration (FDA) recently mandated suicide warnings on antidepressants prescribed to young people. That youth suicide rates have increased since then does not mean the FDA erred in requiring the warnings, argues Alison Bass in the following viewpoint. Adolescents may in fact experience an increase in suicidal thoughts when taking antidepressants, Bass explains. Those who doubt the necessity of the FDA's warnings, in her view, are motivated by their own ties with the pharmaceutical industry. Medical writer Alison Bass authored Side Effects: A Prosecutor, a Whistleblower, and a Bestselling Antidepressant on Trial.

Alison Bass, "Suicide Rates as a Public Relations Tool," *Boston Globe*, September 24, 2007. Copyright © 2007 Globe Newspaper Company. Reproduced by permission of the author.

As you read, consider the following questions:

1. Why did the FDA require black box warnings on antidepressants for youths, as Bass explains it?
2. In the author's assertion, how much did youth suicide rates increase from 2003 to 2004?
3. What might explain the decline in suicides over the last two decades, according to Julie Zito in the viewpoint?

Earlier this month [September 2007], major newspapers reported the alarming news that suicides among young people were on the rise because of a precipitous drop in the use of antidepressants. This news was based on a study in the September issue of the *American Journal of Psychiatry*, which concluded that physicians had been scared away from prescribing antidepressants because of the Food and Drug Administration's decision in October 2004 to put black box warnings on the pediatric use of these drugs. The FDA mandated the warnings after finding an increased risk in suicidal thoughts and behaviors among adolescents taking antidepressants such as Prozac, Zoloft, Paxil, and Celexa.

Responses to the Study

In the wake of the study, several psychiatrists called for the black box warnings to be retracted. "It's time for the agency's warnings to be modified," opined Dr. David Schaffer, chief of child and adolescent psychiatry at Columbia University Medical Center in New York City.

News sources have since exposed a big hole in the journal's argument. Several experts quoted in *The New York Times* and *The Boston Globe* pointed out that while there was indeed an upturn in suicide rates among youths (an increase of 14 percent, or a total of 252 more deaths among youths under 19 between 2003 and 2004), the number of prescriptions for antidepressants in the same age group remained basically unchanged between 2003 and 2004.

The FDA's Antidepressant Medication Guide Warns of Risks for Young People

What is the most important information I should know if my child is being prescribed an antidepressant?

Parents or guardians need to think about 4 important things when their child is prescribed an antidepressant:

1. There is a risk of suicidal thoughts or actions

2. How to try to prevent suicidal thoughts or actions in your child

3. You should watch for certain signs if your child is taking an antidepressant

4. There are benefits and risks when using antidepressants

Children and teenagers sometimes think about suicide, and many report trying to kill themselves.

Antidepressants increase suicidal thoughts and actions in some children and teenagers. But suicidal thoughts and actions can also be caused by depression, a serious medical condition that is commonly treated with antidepressants. Thinking about killing yourself or trying to kill yourself is called *suicidality* or *being suicidal.*

A large study combined the results of 24 different studies of children and teenagers with depression or other illnesses. In these studies, patients took either a placebo (sugar pill) or an antidepressant for 1 to 4 months. *No one committed suicide in these studies,* but some patients became suicidal. On sugar pills, 2 out of every 100 became suicidal. On the antidepressants, 4 out of every 100 patients became suicidal. . . .

FDA, "Medication Guide About Using Antidepressants in Children and Teenagers," January 26, 2005.

According to data presented in the *American Journal of Psychiatry* study, prescription rates for minors did not drop sharply until a year later (between 2004 and 2005). Since suicide rates for 2005 are not yet available from the Centers for Disease Control and Prevention, there is no evidence of a connection between variations in youth suicide rates and antidepressant prescription usage. Furthermore, experts say that trends in suicide rates, like any epidemiological data, have to be looked at over the long term and a one-year variation in rates could be a statistical artifact, or mean something else entirely.

Who Stands to Benefit?

So what's going on here? Why are some in the psychiatric community, despite lack of evidence, working to convince the American public that the FDA may have erred in putting the most serious kind of warning possible on the use of these drugs in young people? In May [2006], the FDA, after finding the same increased risk of suicidal behaviors among young adults taking the class of antidepressants known as selective serotonin reuptake inhibitors (SSRIs), extended the black box warnings to young adults [ages 18 to 24].

There is no doubt that many psychiatrists believe that antidepressants, particularly SSRIs like Prozac, Paxil, Zoloft, and Celexa, are helpful in treating depression in adults and adolescents. They have seen how these drugs have lifted the fog of despair from people with depression.

But there is another factor to consider: Who stands to benefit from the latest alarm about an apparent upturn in youth suicide rates? The sharp drop in the sale of SSRIs since 2004 has put a big dent in their manufacturers' bottom line. These companies have an enormous stake in reversing the current FDA warnings. That might explain why Pfizer (the maker of Zoloft) contributed $30,000 to cover the cost of collecting data for the *American Journal of Psychiatry* study, which was also funded by the National Institute of Mental Health. It's also worth noting that the two lead authors of the paper have disclosed financial conflicts of interest: Columbia professor of psychiatry Dr. John Mann has been a paid consultant to at least two SSRI makers, Pfizer and GlaxoSmithKline (the maker of Paxil), and Robert Gibbons has served as an expert witness for Wyeth Pharmaceuticals (the maker of Effexor, another SSRI).

Skepticism Is Needed

This isn't the first time that suicide rates have been trotted out as a public relations weapon. Proponents of psychotropic drugs have long argued that suicide rates among adults and children fell after the SSRIs were introduced in the United States. However, an examination of long-term trends in suicide rates indicate that suicides were declining here and in other countries well before SSRIs such as Prozac, Zoloft, and Paxil were widely prescribed, says Julie Zito, associate professor of pharmacy and psychiatry at the University of Maryland. Zito says there are other plausible reasons for the decline in suicide rates over the last two decades, including a more stable economy, better access to mental health care, and gun control.

So until new evidence emerges showing, unequivocally, a rising rate of suicides among our youths and a link between those rates and reduced antidepressant usage, it would be wise to treat the latest salvo with a healthy dose of skepticism.

Periodical Bibliography

The following articles have been selected to supplement the diverse views presented in this chapter.

Zagreus Ammon
"Prescription Drugs Without a Doctor," November 14, 2007. http://executive physician.blogspot.com.

Ronald Bailey
"Whose Life Is It Anyway?" *Reason*, March 2, 2007.

Steven P. Cuffe
"Suicide and SSRI Medications in Children and Adolescents: An Update," *DevelopMentor*, Summer 2007. www.aacap.org.

Economist
"Safety in Numbers," March 19, 2005.

FDA Consumer
"From Test Tube to Patient: A Conversation About the FDA and Drug Regulation with Janet Woodcock, MD," January 2006. www.fda.gov.

Jerome Groopman
"The Right to a Trial," *New Yorker*, December 18, 2006.

Louis J. Kraus and Renee Mehlinger
"Black Box Blues: Kids and Antidepressants," *Virtual Mentor*, March 2005.

Las Vegas Review-Journal
"No 'Right' to Save Lives Without the FDA's OK," August 9, 2007.

Courtney E. Martin
"Rethinking Antidepressants and Youth Suicide," *AlterNet*, September 25, 2007. www.alternet.org.

National Consumers League
"Letter to the FDA Regarding Behind the Counter Drugs," December 17, 2007. www.nclnet.org.

George Will
"Go Slow on Bypassing Doc Prescriptions," *Rocky Mountain News*, November 24, 2007.

Walter E. Williams
"FDA: Friend or Foe?" *Human Events*, May 29, 2007. www.humanevents.com.

CHAPTER 3

Are Pharmaceutical Marketing Practices Ethical?

Chapter Preface

One way that pharmaceutical companies identify the doctors most likely to prescribe new drugs and the patients most likely to use them is through data mining. Drugmakers buy detailed prescription information from pharmacies and match it with prescriber data purchased from the American Medical Association (AMA). In this way, they learn which doctors prescribe what drugs and how often. In 2006, New Hampshire became the first state to ban drug companies from buying prescription information for marketing purposes. The companies challenged the legislation, and a federal district court sided with them, overturning the law. Over a dozen states have considered similar bills; one has passed in the Washington State Senate and was in the House of Representatives at press time. Politicians who sponsor these laws are part of a rising tide of criticism aimed at drug companies' marketing practices. Cynics argue that permitting the pharmaceutical industry to purchase prescription information is unethical and a violation of patient privacy codes. The drug industry, on the other hand, contends it has legitimate reasons—and the right—to access prescription data.

Drug sales personnel use data mining to target doctors who write many prescriptions and those who prescribe their competitors' drugs. According to pharmaceutical companies, these doctors benefit from education and updates about drugs they currently prescribe and about new medicines. "When you look at the bigger picture, new therapies often prolong life, increase productivity and diminish costs," maintains Robert Hunkler, a spokesman for IMS Health, which compiles prescription data. Pharmaceutical marketers also use the data to tailor their campaigns to specific patients—for example, those diagnosed with diabetes. Drug developers assert that this right is protected by law, and at least one court agrees. Paul Barbadoro, U.S. district judge, wrote, when striking down the New Hampshire law prohibiting the sale of prescription data for marketing, that the law "restricts speech by preventing pharmaceutical companies from using prescriber-identifiable information both to identify a specific audience for their marketing efforts and to refine their marketing messages." The legislation was unnecessary, the industry claims, because doctors can already opt out of AMA's data sharing and because patients' privacy is preserved. Their names are encrypted before their prescription information is shared, industry supporters point out.

Privacy advocates paint the issue in a much different light. When it comes to providing prescription data to marketers, many doctors echo pediatrician Rupin Thakkar's sentiment: "It feels intrusive. . . . I just feel strongly that medical encounters need to be private." New Hampshire representative Cindy Rosenwald, who sponsored the law that was overruled, reflected on the decision: "In this case, commercial interests took precedence over the interests of the private citizens of New Hampshire. This is like letting a drug rep into an exam room and having them eavesdrop on a private conversation between a physician and a patient." Those who agree with Rosenwald denounce the industry's claim that free speech laws protect its right to access prescription data. Jerry Avorn, author of *Powerful Medicine: The Benefits, Risks, and Costs of Prescription Drugs*, opines, "It seems like a very strange construction of the First Amendment to consider the sale of data about a doctor's prescribing as a kind of free speech." Another complaint voiced by patient advocates is that targeted advertising serves to persuade doctors to prescribe more expensive medicines that may not treat patients effectively.

Drug marketing tactics are especially contentious, as the following chapter reveals. The fervent debate over drug advertising aimed at patients and doctors has brewed for years and will likely not subside any time soon.

| "Drug reps may well have more influence on prescriptions than anyone in America other than doctors themselves."

Drug Detailing Greatly Influences Doctors' Prescribing Habits

Carl Elliott

In detailing, sales personnel visit doctors to provide information about drugs and offer samples. Carl Elliott contends in the following viewpoint that detailing convinces doctors to write prescriptions for drugs that may be toxic or less effective than others on the market. He claims that drug representatives are paid according to how many prescriptions they convince physicians to write. So, they form personal relationships with doctors and give them gifts, the author contends, and he says this induces a sense of reciprocity. Carl Elliott, an author of several books on medicine and morality, teaches at University of Minnesota's Center for Bioethics.

As you read, consider the following questions:

1. According to Elliott, how does the return on each dollar spent on detailing compare to the return on direct-to-consumer advertising?

Carl Elliott, "The Drug Pushers," *Atlantic Monthly*, vol. 297, April 2006, pp. 82–93. Reproduced by permission of the author.

2. In what ways do doctors differ from drug reps, in the author's contention?

3. How does Elliott describe "Northeast-Southwest" tactics?

Back in the old days, long before drug companies started making headlines in the business pages, doctors were routinely called upon by company representatives known as "detail men." To "detail" a doctor is to give that doctor information about a company's new drugs, with the aim of persuading the doctor to prescribe them. When I was growing up, in South Carolina in the 1970s, I would occasionally see detail men sitting patiently in the waiting room outside the office of my father, a family doctor. They were pretty easy to spot. Detail men were usually sober, conservatively dressed gentlemen who would not have looked out of place at the Presbyterian church across the street. Instead of Bibles or hymn books, though, they carried detail bags, which were filled with journal articles, drug samples, and branded knickknacks for the office.

The Modern-Day Drug Rep

Today detail men are officially known as "pharmaceutical sales representatives," but everyone I know calls them "drug reps." Drug reps are still easy to spot in a clinic or hospital, but for slightly different reasons. The most obvious is their appearance. It is probably fair to say that doctors, pharmacists, and medical-school professors are not generally admired for their good looks and fashion sense. Against this backdrop, the average drug rep looks like a supermodel, or maybe an A-list movie star. Drug reps today are often young, well groomed, and strikingly good-looking. Many are women. They are usually affable and sometimes very smart. Many give off a kind of glow, as if they had just emerged from a spa or salon. And they are always, hands down, the best-dressed people in the hospital.

Drug reps have been calling on doctors since the mid-nineteenth century, but during the past decade or so their numbers have increased dramatically. From 1996 to 2001 the pharmaceutical sales force in America doubled, to a total of 90,000 reps. One reason is simple: good reps move product. Detailing is expensive, but almost all practicing doctors see reps at least occasionally, and many doctors say they find reps useful. One study found that for drugs introduced after 1997 with revenues exceeding $200 million a year, the average return for each dollar spent on detailing was $10.29. That is an impressive figure. It is almost twice the return on investment in medical-journal advertising, and more than seven times the return on direct-to-consumer advertising.

But the relationship between doctors and drug reps has never been uncomplicated, for reasons that should be obvious. The first duty of doctors, at least in theory, is to their patients. Doctors must make prescribing decisions based on medical evidence and their own clinical judgment. Drug reps, in contrast, are salespeople. They swear no oaths, take care of no patients, and profess no high-minded ethical duties. Their job is to persuade doctors to prescribe their drugs. If reps are lucky, their drugs are good, the studies are clear, and their job is easy. But sometimes reps must persuade doctors to prescribe drugs that are marginally effective, exorbitantly expensive, difficult to administer, or even dangerously toxic. Reps that succeed are rewarded with bonuses or commissions. Reps that fail may find themselves unemployed.

They're Difficult to Demonize

Most people who work in health care, if they give drug reps any thought at all, regard them with mixed feelings. A handful avoid reps as if they were vampires, backing out of the room when they see one approaching. In their view, the best that can be said about reps is that they are a necessary by-product of a market economy. They view reps much as NBA players used to view Michael Jordan: as an awesome, powerful force that you can never really stop, only hope to control.

Yet many reps are so friendly, so easygoing, so much fun to flirt with that it is virtually impossible to demonize them. How can you, demonize someone who brings you lunch and touches your arm and remembers your birthday and knows the names of all your children? After awhile even the most steel-willed doctors may look forward to visits by a rep, if only in the self-interested way that they look forward to the UPS truck pulling up in their driveway. A rep at the door means a delivery has arrived: take-out for the staff, trinkets for the kids, and, most indispensably, drug samples on the house. Although samples are the single largest marketing expense for the drug industry, they pay handsome dividends: doctors who accept samples of a drug are far more likely to prescribe that drug later on.

Drug reps may well have more influence on prescriptions than anyone in America other than doctors themselves. . . .

More Prescriptions = Bigger Paycheck

For most reps, market share is the yardstick of success. The more scripts their doctors write for their drugs, the more the reps make. [Former drug rep Kathleen] Slattery-Moschkau says that most of her fellow reps made $50,000 to $90,000 a year in salary and another $30,000 to $50,000 in bonuses, depending on how much they sold. Reps are pressured to "make quota," or meet yearly sales targets, which often increase from year to year. Reps who fail to make quota must endure the indignity of having their district manager frequently accompany them on sales calls. Those who meet quota are rewarded handsomely. The most successful reps achieve minor celebrity within the company.

One perennial problem for reps is the doctor who simply refuses to see them at all. Reps call these doctors "No Sees." Cracking a No See is a genuine achievement, the pharmaceu-

Drug Reps Should Be Prohibited from Giving Doctors Gifts

Because gifts of even minimal value carry influence and because disclosure is an inadequate safeguard, the guidance presently provided by the medical profession, the pharmaceutical industry, and the federal government fails to protect the best interests of patients and the integrity of physician decision making. For these reasons, many current practices should be prohibited and others should be more strictly regulated to eliminate potential sources of unwarranted influence.

All gifts (zero dollar limit), free meals, payment for time for travel to or time at meetings, and payment for participation in online CME [Continuing Medical Education] from drug and medical device companies to physicians should be prohibited. A complete ban on these activities by eliminating potential gray areas greatly eases the burden of compliance. It also frees physicians from deciding whether a gift is appropriate and removes a principal mode by which detail persons gain access to physicians' offices and influence their decision making.

Troyen A. Brennan et al.,
Journal of the American Medical Association,
January 25, 2006.

tical equivalent of a home run or a windmill dunk. [Ex-drug Marketer] Gene Carbona says that when he came across a No See, or any other doctor who was hard to influence, he used "Northeast-Southwest" tactics. If you can't get to a doctor, he explains, you go after the people surrounding that doctor, showering them with gifts. Carbona might help support a Little League baseball team or a bowling league. After awhile, the doctor would think, Gene is doing such nice things for all these people, the least I can do is give him ten minutes of my time. At that point, Carbona says, the sale was as good as made. "If you could get ten minutes with a doctor, your market share would go through the roof."

Doctors Are Not Incorruptible

For decades the medical community has debated whether gifts and perks from reps have any real effect. Doctors insist that they do not. Studies in the medical literature indicate just the opposite. Doctors who take gifts from a company, studies show, are more likely to prescribe that company's drugs or ask that they be added to their hospital's formulary. The pharmaceutical industry has managed this debate skillfully, pouring vast resources into gifts for doctors while simultaneously reassuring them that their integrity prevents them from being influenced. For example, in a recent editorial in the journal *Health Affairs*, Bert Spilker, a vice president for PhRMA, the pharmaceutical trade group, defended the practice of gift-giving against critics who, he scornfully wrote, "fear that physicians are so weak and lacking in integrity that they would 'sell their souls' for a pack of M&M candies and a few sandwiches and doughnuts."

Doctors' belief in their own incorruptibility appears to be honestly held. It is rare to hear a doctor—even in private, off-the-record conversation—admit that industry gifts have made a difference in his or her prescribing. In fact, according to one small study of medical residents in the *Canadian Medical Association Journal*, one way to convince doctors that they cannot be influenced by gifts may be to give them one; the more gifts a doctor takes, the more likely that doctor is to believe that the gifts have had no effect. This helps explain why it makes sense for reps to give away even small gifts. A particular gift may have no influence, but it might make a doctor more apt to think that he or she would not be influenced by larger gifts in the future. A pizza and a penlight are like inoculations, tiny injections of self-confidence that make a doctor think, I will never be corrupted by money.

Gifts from the drug industry are nothing new, of course. William Helfand, who worked in marketing for Merck for thirty-three years, told me that company representatives were giving doctors books and pamphlets as early as the late nineteenth century. "There is nothing new under the sun," Helfand says. "There is just more of it."

"Physicians are tough sells, in that the effect of sales force activity on prescribing behavior is modest."

Drug Detailing Has Little Influence on Doctors' Prescribing Habits

Natalie Mizik and Robert Jacobson

Pharmaceutical sales representatives (PSRs) often visit doctor offices to promote drugs and distribute samples in interactions known as detailing. According to the following viewpoint, excerpted from a study by Natalie Mizik and Robert Jacobson, PSR detailing is unlikely to persuade physicians to prescribe drugs. The authors explain that doctors are skeptical of sales personnel and do not pay them credence. Mizik and Jacobson discovered only small increases in prescriptions written after detailing, leading them to surmise that it has limited influence on doctors. Mizik is a business professor at Columbia University and Jacobson is a marketing professor at University of Washington.

Natalie Mizik and Robert Jacobson, "Are Physicians 'Easy Marks'? Quantifying the Effects of Detailing and Sampling on New Prescriptions," *Management Science*, vol. 50, December 2004, pp. 1704–1707, 1714. Copyright © 2007 INFORMS, Institute for Operations Research and the Management Sciences. All rights reserved. Reproduced by permission.

As you read, consider the following questions:

1. According to Mizik and Jacobson, what are the two opposing views on PSRs' influence on physicians?
2. What four influences are far more important to doctors than PSRs, in Mizik and Jacobson's assertion?
3. How many more samples of drug B would need to be given to doctors before one new prescription would be generated, according to the authors?

As the cost of prescription drugs continues to escalate, increased public attention is being focused on the marketing practices of the pharmaceutical firms as one source of the problem. Direct-to-physician activities account for the bulk of U.S. pharmaceutical firm promotional spending. IMS Health (2003) estimates that over $5.8 billion was spent in 2002 on detailing, i.e., pharmaceutical sales representatives (PSRs) visiting physicians to promote their firm's drugs. In addition, the retail value of the free drug samples distributed during these visits is estimated at $11.5 billion.

A detailing visit typically lasts two to five minutes during which time a PSR discusses one to three of the company's drugs. Information (and, at times, misinformation) about a drug's composition, therapeutic value, proper dosage, and potential side effects is communicated. Often, PSRs will also dispense samples and possibly offer small gifts to the physician. At issue is whether these interactions with PSRs compromise physician integrity and affect their prescribing behavior. More precisely, the key public policy issue is the extent to which the industry's promotional tactics lead to an increase in appropriate versus inappropriate use of drugs in a cost-effective manner. . . .

The Impact of Drug Detailing:
Negative or Positive?

Two competing views have dominated discussion on the matter. The prevailing view contends that PSRs significantly influence physicians' prescribing behavior and that this influence has negative effect on patients' welfare, in that PSRs encourage physicians to prescribe more expensive branded drugs. Many public policy organizations and consumer advocacy groups adhere to this view. The prominent alternative view argues that PSRs do influence physicians' prescribing behavior, but that this influence is positive in that PSRs provide physicians with valuable information. As a result, physicians are better informed and make better choices for their patients. Pharmaceutical companies and industry groups advocate this second view.

Despite the substantial resources that pharmaceutical companies invest in promoting their products and the controversy associated with pharmaceutical marketing practices, surprisingly little is known about the magnitude of the impact that PSR visits and free drug samples have on physician prescribing behavior. [A marketing professor at Stanford, Sridhar] Narayanan [and his coauthors] (2003) report a pharmaceutical executive as stating, "No one is really sure if sending the legions of reps to doctors' offices really works. Everyone is afraid to stop it, because they don't know what difference it's making."

In point of fact, much of the evidence on PSR effectiveness is anecdotal. The empirical studies investigating the issue have been subject to data or methodological limitations that restricted their ability to control for potential biases and have come to contradictory conclusions regarding even the central issues: the effects of detailing on prescriptions, of detailing on price elasticity, and even of price on sales.

We have obtained access to a unique database that allows us to undertake econometric analysis that overcomes a number of fundamental limitations existing in past research. . . . The large number of observations in the database (it involves a total of more than 2 million observations) allows us to accurately pinpoint the impact that interactions with PSRs have on the number of new prescriptions issued by physicians.

We find that, although detailing and free drug samples have a positive and statistically significant association with the number of new prescriptions issued by a physician, the magnitudes of the effects are modest. As such, our results challenge the two dominant views and support the contention that, rather than being easy marks, physicians are tough sells. This realization is important because the public policy debate continues over how best to address the high cost of prescription drugs.

PSR Influence on Physicians Is Limited

Most discussions of PSRs have focused on the factors facilitating their influence. Unquestionably, PSRs provide physicians with information about new drugs, new indications, dosages, and interactions for existing medicines. [Massachusetts Institute of Technology professor Pierre] Azoulay (2002) finds evidence that detailing diffuses product information. [Harvard professor Jerry] Avorn [and his colleagues] (1982) report that 20% of surveyed physicians view information provided by PSRs as "very important" in influencing their prescribing behavior. Furthermore, PSRs are trained in persuading physicians. Detailing takes the form of presenting facts and, as has been documented, misrepresenting facts about the drug in an effective manner. Finally, mere exposure or salience effects might lead to a temporary increase in prescribing following a PSR visit. Numerous studies have reported high physician responsiveness to PSR activity attributed it to PSR persuasiveness.

Less attention has been paid to the factors limiting PSR effectiveness. The key consideration here is that PSRs are not the only or even the primary source of information about drugs for physicians. Scientific papers, advice from colleagues, and a physician's own training and experience also influence prescribing practices. Indeed, most physicians view these other influences as far more important than that of PSRs.

PSR influence is limited by the fact that many physicians have skeptical or negative attitudes toward PSRs. Attribution theory suggests that with low source credibility, which is determined by factors such as a source's trustworthiness and expertise, arguments in a message will be discounted. Physicians recognize that PSRs are neither experts nor completely trustworthy. They realize that information presented is biased toward the promoted drug and is unlikely to be objective or even accurate. Thus, physicians will discount information received from a PSR.

Some additional characteristics of physicians would seem to make them particularly tough sells. [Marketing professors Marian] Friestad and [Peter] Wright's (1994) persuasion knowledge model suggests that targets of persuasion use their knowledge about the persuasion agent and can effectively cope with and even achieve their own goals during a persuasion attempt, e.g., obtaining free drug samples that can be later distributed to patients. [Margaret] Campbell and [Amna] Kirmani's (2000) tests of the persuasion knowledge model reveal that busy targets with accessible agent motivation (a profile that would fit most physicians) are particularly effective in resisting persuasion.

When cast within the workings of other sources of influence, we would expect the ability of PSRs to influence physician behavior to be relatively small. . . .

Study Results

Access to the data was gained from a U.S. pharmaceutical manufacturer with the only condition of ensuring the anonymity of the firm and the drugs in the study. Two different sets of data were merged to form the database. One data set pertains to the number of new prescriptions for the studied drugs and their competitors issued by physicians during a month. The *new prescription* measure reflects both new and repeat usage, but does not reflect refills accompanying the prescriptions. These data cover a 24-month period for three widely prescribed drugs. The second data set pertains to detailing and sampling activity by PSRs for the same three drugs. The two data sets were merged into one database containing prescribing and promotional activity information by month and physician. . . .

The focus of our study was to assess the magnitude of physician responsiveness to two main pharmaceutical marketing practices while controlling for other possible influences on prescribing. Our results show that physicians are tough sells, in that the effect of sales force activity on prescribing behavior is modest. For the three drugs in our study the estimated total effects on new prescriptions are 1.56, 0.32, and 0.153 for detailing and 0.155, 0.039, and 0.014 for sampling. In other words, for the three drugs in our study it would take an additional 0.64, 3.13, and 6.54 PSR visits, respectively, to induce one additional new prescription for the drugs. It would take 6.44, 25.64, and 73.04 additional free drug samples to induce one additional new prescription.

The high statistical significance of the estimates indicates that these marketing activities have an effect on the new prescriptions, but the magnitude of the effect indicates that PSR activities have only a modest impact. . . .

Given the modest response to PSR activity, the question is no longer "Are physicians easy marks?" but rather "Why do drug companies make such extensive use of PSRs, given their limited effectiveness?" It appears that drug company profits might be enhanced (or drug prices reduced) through cost savings achieved through a reduction in PSR numbers. Although this might be true, some additional issues need to be considered. First, it should be remembered that our estimates reflect the effect of a visit on the sales of a single drug. A PSR might discuss more than one drug during a visit, so the impact of a given visit will be greater than its effect on a single drug. Second, the reported estimates relate to new prescriptions issued. Sales of the drug, however, will also be based on the refills accompanying the prescription, which average between two and three for the drugs in our study. Both these considerations magnify the financial implications of a detailing visit. Furthermore, the margin to the pharmaceutical firm on a drug can be considerable. Based on these considerations, we believe that the returns to detailing of Drug A are positive, which stems both from its larger margin and the larger estimated physician response to detailing, whereas returns to detailing of Drug B and of Drug C are negative.

Why would the firms persist at engaging in a practice that has negative returns? Indeed, the number of PSRs continues to increase and is now over 85,000; it has almost doubled in the past five years [from 1999 to 2004] although the number of physicians has remained constant. Our results suggest that for some drugs (e.g., those with lower margins) the current detailing system is suboptimal. This situation might be a result of the intensive PSR "arms race" the pharmaceutical industry has undertaken. A recent McKinsey report questions the effectiveness of the current PSR system and advocates that pharmaceutical companies transform their sales model.

"*It is a fact of life that direct-to-consumer (DTC) promotion has become increasingly educational. . . .*"

Direct-to-Consumer Drug Marketing Educates Patients

Sal Perreca

In the following viewpoint, Sal Perreca outlines the benefits of direct-to-consumer (DTC) advertising, especially with its recent emphasis on education. Perreca says that DTC advertising ensures that patients are properly informed on products so they can ask their physicians questions and become more involved in the decision-making process. He says it is important for companies to make a concentrated effort to focus their advertising on consumer education, and that self-regulation is an important step in the process. Sal Perreca is chairman and CEO of Lowe HealthCare Worldwide.

As you read, consider the following questions:

1. According the viewpoint, why can a complex ad backfire?

2. In the author's view, whose responsibility is it to maximize patient education?

Sal Perreca, "Long Live Consumer Education (Back Talk)," *Medical Marketing & Media*, vol. 41, July 2006, p. 190. Copyright © 2006 Haymarket Media, Inc. Reproduced by permission.

3. What does Perreca think is central to restoring public confidence?

It is a fact of life that direct-to-consumer (DTC) promotion has become increasingly educational—as addressed by PhRMA's guidelines for DTC advertising, FDA's public hearing on consumer guidelines and, recently, the Coalition for Healthcare Communication's citizens' petition.

Pharma, medical education providers and practitioners will all be focused on compliance and safety, with drug companies seeking assurance that providers will follow the same regulations by which they are governed. This is a trend we will see more of in 2006–07—redirecting dollars away from branded Rx campaigns to unbranded and educational efforts.

Start by Educating the Doctors

So how do we respond? This shift represents a platform for agencies to work together with pharma to ensure that physicians are properly informed on products before patients begin asking questions, and that the consumer is educated on efficacy and safety. A DTC campaign that catches the doctor off-guard can boomerang, and in a highly competitive marketplace it can discourage prescribing.

PhRMA's guidelines for a delay between product launch and DTC advertising is actually a tremendous timing opportunity for pharma and their agencies. It can be a period used to fully integrate the messages that are being given to physicians with the data being given to consumers. The education process starts with the doctor—to both inform and ensure that the doctor has the complete efficacy and safety picture before a consumer campaign is launched.

We all know that the glut of warning information appended to a consumer ad is often misunderstood or ignored due to the sheer volume or complexity of the warning. To help properly educate the consumer, agencies and their clients

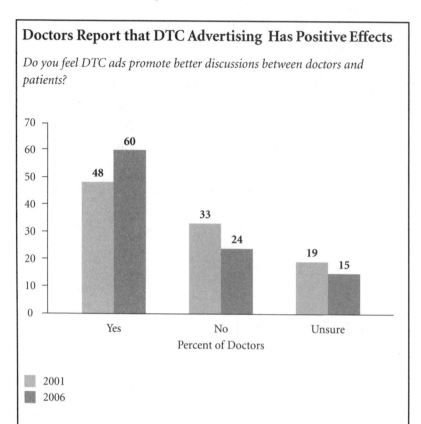

Doctors Report that DTC Advertising Has Positive Effects

Do you feel DTC ads promote better discussions between doctors and patients?

2001
2006

TAKEN FROM: Albert W. Morris, Jr., et al., "For the Good of the Patient: Survey of the Physicians of the National Medical Association Regarding Perceptions of DTC Advertising, Part II, 2006," *Journal of the National Medical Association, 2007.*

can provide tools to facilitate patient-physician communication, with an end goal being the sharing of concise, comprehensive and useful therapeutic and disease-state data for the both patient and physician. The venues for educating can include the sales force, direct mail and the internet, as well as journal advertising.

A New Generation of Patients

It is up to the agency and pharma to maximize this patient education. The ultimate patient-education goal is to share information effectively with the consumer to enhance understanding of his or her disease-state, treatment, drug efficacy and safety issues. This education effort goes a long way towards creating a knowledgeable, well-informed patient, who is able to collaborate with doctors and caregivers. A new generation of physicians has evolved who recognize this and have become more proactive in getting their patients involved in decision-making processes related to their own care.

Making a concerted effort to comprehensively and earnestly educate the consumer can go a long way in allowing pharma to reclaim the high ground and some semblance of the integrity that has been lost over the past five years. A dose of higher standards and a clear and public focus on patient safety can only help an industry that is in danger of becoming a byword for inflated revenues.

Self-regulation is a small, first step toward improving our collective image. A self-imposed delay on DTC campaigns, increased safety warnings and timely relaying of developing issues can demonstrate how the industry is proactively taking steps to ensure patient safety. An industry-wide focus on safety and patient/consumer education is central to restoring public confidence.

Consumer education—bring it on.

"*[Direct-to-consumer advertising] may also have negative economic, social, and political consequences.*"

Direct-to-Consumer Drug Marketing Harms Patients

Peter R. Mansfield

In the following viewpoint, Peter R. Mansfield disparages direct-to-consumer advertising (DTCA) of drugs. In his view, such advertising is deleterious because it persuades people to take medications that are so new the risks have not yet been realized. Furthermore, the author maintains, DTCA makes people anxious or unhappy about normal life experiences, leading them to use prescription drugs unnecessarily. He alleges that DTCA also ratchets up costs and provides unreliable or incomplete information under the auspices of being informative. Peter R. Mansfield is a general practitioner and director of the Web site Healthy Skepticism, which fights against the misleading promotion of drugs.

As you read, consider the following questions:

1. In Mansfield's assertion, what types of high-priority health messages are minimized by DTCA?

Elizabeth A. Almasi, Randall S. Stafford, Richard L. Kravitz, and Peter R. Mansfield, "What Are the Public Health Effects of Direct-to-Consumer Drug Advertising?" *PLoS Medicine*, vol. 3, no. 3, March 2006, pp. 286–287. Copyright © Almasi et al. Reproduced by permission.

2. How does DTC marketing increase the cost of drugs, as the author explains it?

3. In Mansfield's opinion, what are the two main problems with DTCA?

The collective evidence on DTCA [direct-to-consumer advertising] suggests that it may have some benefits, but there is stronger evidence of harms. Greater benefit could be gained, with less harm, from publicly funded health information and promotion.

New Drugs Are Highly Profitable

DTCA is limited to drugs that are profitable to advertise: mostly expensive, new drugs for long-term use for common indications. Such advertising increases premature rapid uptake and overuse of new drugs before flaws, including safety problems, have been discovered and communicated to health professionals. Many new drugs are inferior to older treatments, and over two-thirds are no better but are often more expensive. Increased use of new drugs stimulated by DTCA can lead to adverse events directly (for example, cardiovascular events associated with COX-2 selective inhibitors, which were heavily advertised to the US public) or indirectly, by diverting resources from more cost-effective interventions.

DTCA rarely focuses on, and tends to drown out, high-priority public health messages about diet, exercise, addictions, social involvement, equity, pollution, climate change, and appropriate use of older drugs. Older drugs are less profitable to advertise because a share of the sales stimulated goes to generic competition. Consequently, DTCA for any currently advertised drug will become less profitable after expiry of patent protection from competition. When DTCA no longer provides competitive return on investment, it is stopped. Consequently, if there are any benefits from current DTCA (such as stimulating new requests for statins after a myocardial infarction), those benefits will be for a limited time only.

DTC Advertising Takes the Focus Away from Real Health Concerns

DTC [direct-to-consumer] ads distort the relationship between patients and clinicians. DTC ads manipulate the patient's agenda and steal precious time away from an evidence-based primary care clinician agenda that is attempting to promote healthy behavior, screen for early-stage treatable disease, and address mental health. The negative consequences of this manipulation of the public, the patient, the clinician, and their relationship are subtle but pervasive. An insidious adverse effect occurs in what is not done during the limited time of a visit. Discussing why the advertised drug is not the best option for a particular patient may mean that a mammogram is not ordered, an important health behavior is not discussed, a family matter is not brought up, a deeper patient concern is never articulated, a diagnosis for which there is no drug ad is not made. The clinician is put in the role of gatekeeper for the advertised commodity rather than a gateway for prioritizing health care based on the concerns of patients and the science-based recommendations for preventive, chronic disease, mental health, and family care.

Kurt C. Stange,
Annals of Family Medicine, *March–April 2007.*

The Ultimate Persuasion

DTCA aims to persuade rather than to inform, and there is evidence that it is effective at persuasion. Content analyses of DTCA have found that the information provided is usually flawed and incomplete. Examples include a study of 320 drug advertisements in popular US magazines that found that the advertisements rarely provided information about success rates of treatment or alternative treatments, and a study of 23 US television advertisements for prescription drugs that found that the majority gave more time to benefits than to risks.

Such advertising can lead some people to falsely believe they are well informed, so it reduces their motivation to search for more reliable information. Finding reliable information is already difficult (like finding a needle in a haystack) and the "noise" of DTCA just makes the haystack larger.

Advertising drugs to the public often works by creating or exacerbating unhappiness or anxiety about symptoms or normal experiences (such as occasional erectile difficulties), and by creating high expectations of benefit from drugs. The combination of heightened unhappiness and high expectations can cause severe distress when a drug is unaffordable or when its effects are disappointing: for example, a qualitative study of men who used sildenafil for erectile dysfunction found that expectations raised by media hyperbole had an adverse effect on the morale of those for whom it was ineffective.

DTCA is often ambiguous and widens the indications beyond those for which the promoted drugs are worthwhile. For example, DTCA may have contributed to increasing unjustified use of antidepressants for young people.

DTCA may also have negative economic, social, and political consequences. For example, by increasing use of expensive drugs and increasing adverse events, DTCA increases taxpayer, insurance, and individual costs, which in turn can harm individual, familial, and national economies. The heavy costs of DTCA contribute to higher drug prices and are a hurdle for market entry of new competition. Revenue from DTCA creates a conflict of interest for media companies, because such advertising can undermine the media's freedom to report critically on the drug industry. DTCA can have a distorting effect on people's perceptions of health and disease, including promoting the medicalization of conditions that are within the spectrum of normality. DTCA sometimes persuades people to interpret distress as signifying individual illness rather than social or political problems to be solved. DTCA pushes a "Brave New World" where if "anything unpleasant should somehow happen, why, there's always [the sedative] soma to give you a holiday from the facts. And there's always soma to calm your anger, to reconcile you to your enemies, to make you patient and long-suffering".

How to Address These Problems

There are two root causes of the problems with DTCA. The first is payment systems that reward drug companies for increasing sales of expensive drugs regardless of the impact on health. These systems should be redesigned. The second root cause is normal human vulnerability to being misled. Few people have the time and advanced skills in drug evaluation, psychology, logic, economics, and semiotics, etc., required to evaluate drug promotion. Advertising can sneak in under the radar to influence even skeptical people without their awareness. Ideas that would be rejected if given attention get reinforced by repetition. More research is needed to test the hypothesis that it is possible to learn how to gain more benefit than harm when exposed to drug promotion.

Almost all government, health professional, and consumer inquiries into DTCA have concluded that it causes net public harm. It is too difficult to regulate DTCA, so I believe that the logical conclusion from the evidence is that the best option for improving overall health and wealth is to ban all types of DTCA, including "disease awareness" advertising. Drug company Web sites and media releases should be regulated carefully.

The public would benefit from reliable information and health promotion focused on public health priorities. Such information can be provided at no extra cost by copying, improving, and expanding policies and programs that are already successful in many countries. Governments and insurance companies who subsidize drugs currently pay for biased promotion indirectly via high drug prices. Instead, these agencies could fund information, education, and promotional services focused on public health needs. Such investments pay for themselves by reducing health care costs. Universities and nonprofit organizations are well placed to compete for this funding. These organizations are more trustworthy than drug companies because they don't gain from drug sales. Where behavior-change promotion is justified, these organizations could collaborate with advertising agencies. This collaborative approach has already been successful for many health-promotion campaigns—for example, promoting smoking cessation. These improvements would not achieve utopia, but would improve health and increase wealth overall.

"Pharmaceutical research companies . . . naturally have the most thorough information and . . . their representatives are well-prepared to explain medicines."

Drug Manufacturers' Efforts to Educate Doctors Are Legitimate and Ethical

The Pharmaceutical Research and Manufacturers of America

The Pharmaceutical Research and Manufacturers of America (PhRMA), a group of drug research and biotechnology companies, promotes drug innovation. In the following viewpoint, PhRMA makes assurances that its companies' sales representatives are trained to supply doctors with valuable information about medicines, their benefits, and side effects. Such education, it avows, is accurate, does not affect doctors' ability to make independent judgments about medicines, and should not be restricted. PhRMA maintains that both its code and its federal regulations ensure that relationships between drug marketers and doctors are ethical. The code specifies, for instance, that providing doctors lavish meals while discussing medications is inappropriate, PhRMA points out.

As you read, consider the following questions:

1. From what sources should physicians obtain information about drugs, according to PhRMA?

2. In the author's opinion, when is it appropriate for sales personnel to bring doctors meals?

3. How do free drug samples benefit patients, as PhRMA explains it?

Pharmaceutical Research and Manufacturers of America (PhRMA) Senior Vice President Ken Johnson issued the following statement today [February 13, 2007] on attempts to restrict or ban discussions between technically-trained drug sales representatives and health professionals:

"America's pharmaceutical research companies strongly agree that the prescribing decisions of all health care practitioners should be based on the best medical and scientific evidence and a patient's individual needs.

"That's why we advocate physicians and other health professionals obtaining information about medicines from a wide range of sources, including medical journals, continuing medical education courses, other physicians and the technically-trained sales representatives of the pharmaceutical research companies that discover and develop new treatments. Most health professionals review information from different sources and make independent decisions.

"Sales representatives—many of whom are health care professionals themselves—are well-prepared to provide the latest scientific information about the medicines developed by their research-based companies. And they can answer an array of questions about drugs and their characteristics, including queries about the benefits, proper use and side effects of the treatments. America's pharmaceutical research companies—which generated tens of thousands of pages of scientific data as they researched and developed new drugs—naturally have the most thorough information and they make sure their representatives are well-prepared to explain medicines and their features."

Interactions Between Sales Representatives and Physicians Are Well-Governed

"The Food and Drug Administration provides the regulatory teeth to make sure information provided by sales representatives is accurate and well-balanced. Companies must comply with strict agency regulations. Additionally, the effort to guarantee accuracy and balance is boosted by PhRMA itself through its voluntary marketing guidelines, which are contained in its Code on Interactions with Healthcare Professionals. The comprehensive PhRMA marketing code provides guidance on how sales personnel can and should maintain ethical relationships in their discussions with health care professionals.

"The PhRMA Code is designed to ensure that the focus of interactions between sales representatives and physicians is the valuable information the reps provide about drugs and how they work. The guidelines state that lavish meals, entertainment—including sporting events—and expensive gifts are never appropriate. Gifts that may be appropriate under the Code should support the medical practices of health professionals.

"Specifically, meals are supposed to be modest. While sales representatives do not have a vested interest in bringing food to physicians' offices, the fact is that doctors and other health professionals are very busy and often the only time they have to meet to discuss medicines is over a working lunch or dinner. The PhRMA Code contemplates modest meals only if they are provided during presentations about the benefits, risks and proper use of drugs."

The Pharmaceutical Industry's Marketing Code Ensures That Drug Education Is Accurate and Ethical

The ethical promotion of prescription medicines is vital to the pharmaceutical industry's mission of helping patients by discovering, developing and marketing new medicines. Ethical promotion helps to ensure that health care professionals have access to information they need, that patients have access to the medicines they need and that medicines are prescribed and used in a manner that provides the maximum health care benefit to patients.

IFPMA [International Federation of Pharmaceutical Manufacturers & Associations] and its members are committed to educational and promotional efforts that benefit patients and promotional programs and collaborations that enhance the practice of medicine. IFPMA also seeks to preserve the independence of the decisions taken by health care professionals in prescribing medicines to patients. The pharmaceutical industry has an obligation and responsibility to provide accurate information and education about its products to health care professionals in order to establish a clear understanding of the appropriate use of prescription medicines. Industry relationships with health care professionals must support, and be consistent with, the professional responsibilities health care professionals have towards their patients. Pharmaceutical companies must maintain high ethical standards when conducting promotional activities and comply with applicable legal, regulatory and professional requirements. Through the promotion of this Code, IFPMA seeks to ensure that ethical promotional practices are established worldwide.

International Federation of Pharmaceutical Manufacturers & Associations,
IFPMA Code of Pharmaceutical Marketing Practices, *2006.*

Valuable Benefits

"Clearly, today's meetings between sales representatives and doctors do not hinder the ability of physicians to make independent judgments. But because it is important health professionals receive the crucial technical drug data companies can provide, PhRMA members are interested in learning about other ways of providing the latest scientific information about medicines researched and developed by biopharmaceutical companies. PhRMA does not think that the answers lie in medical schools, hospitals and clinics that restrict the access of pharmaceutical sales representatives as this could limit—or cut off altogether—vital information about the benefits and risks of new medicines.

"When addressing the free patient samples companies provide, it is important to remember the benefit that samples bring to patients and their doctors. For physicians, samples help them receive early hands-on experience to determine if certain treatments are going to benefit the patients in their medical practices. For patients, it is a matter of having doctors who have the information they need to make the right treatment decisions. In addition, free samples are often given to uninsured patients who cannot afford their medications.

"In the end, it all boils down to helping make certain patients are safely and effectively treated. Pharmaceutical marketing is one of several important ways for doctors to receive the information they need to make sure their treatment choices are the right ones and their patients are properly treated."

"It is the job of medical schools and their faculty . . . to educate doctors. . . . To abdicate that responsibility is wrong."

Drug Manufacturers' Efforts to Educate Doctors Are Unethical

Marcia Angell

In the following viewpoint, Marcia Angell denounces education administered by drug company representatives. In her opinion, pharmaceutical companies cannot be expected to provide physicians unbiased information about drugs. In fact, Angell charges that drugmakers claim the information, payments, and gifts they offer doctors are part of an educational, not marketing, campaign to evade bribery laws and skirt guidelines that allow such activities only if they serve an educational purpose. The medical industry must take responsibility for educating doctors, she insists. Angell is a physician and proponent of medical reform who was named one of Time *magazine's twenty-five most influential people in America.*

As you read, consider the following questions:

1. How many events that Angell calls "pseudo-educational" were hosted in 2000?

2. In what three ways does medical education pay, according to the author?

3. What does medical education "worthy of the name" require, in Angell's opinion?

Drug companies are extremely generous to doctors in their "educational" activities. The education is often said to go in both directions. The companies provide information to doctors, and the doctors provide feedback to the companies. But the money goes in only one direction—from industry to doctors. Doctors are invited to dinners in expensive restaurants or on junkets to luxurious settings to act as "consultants" or "advisers." The doctors listen to speakers and provide some minimal response about how they like the company drugs or what they think of a new advertising campaign. That enables drug companies to pay doctors just for showing up. As one doctor told *The Boston Globe*, "The companies used to call it coming to dinner. Now it's called consulting."

Participants may also receive training to serve on speakers' bureaus, so that they, too, can become company shills. The work on junkets is not too onerous. Lectures usually occupy just a few hours in the morning, with plenty of time left for golf or skiing in the afternoon and elegant meals and entertainment in the evenings. By calling it education or consulting or market research or some combination of those things, but *not* marketing, companies needn't worry about antikickback laws [which make bribing doctors to prescribe drugs illegal]. But doctors are no less beholden to the companies that lavish such attention on them, and they are no more immune to the sales pitches. It's been estimated that the industry hosted over 300,000 pseudo-educational events in 2000, about a quarter of

Drug Companies Carefully Control the Information Doctors Receive About Pharmaceuticals

Drug companies are subtle. They not only provide gifts and dinners and seminars, but also leave behind carefully selected studies that support the use of their drugs. The overarching goal is to control the information that doctors receive about medications.

Drug companies write the package inserts of all drugs, carefully including the information they choose and omitting information they want to avoid. Drug companies underwrite a large percentage of continuing education courses for doctors. In doing so, they make sure that the speakers represent the company view.... Drug reps typically bring stacks of studies, all favorable, which impress doctors.... Drug reps do not include independent studies with less favorable conclusions. Many doctors never see these.

Jay S. Cohen, MedicationSense, *January–April 2006.*
www.medicationsense.com.

which offered continuing medical education credits [which doctors need to keep their licenses]....

Pretending Drug Companies Are Educators

Why do doctors pretend they believe drug companies are interested in education? (Some of them may actually believe it.) The answer is: It pays. Membership dues would be far higher if professional societies were not supported by industry. Doctors would also have to pay for their own continuing medical education. In addition, they would lose the travel and entertainment and other emoluments too many of them have come to believe are entitlements of their profession. Many doctors become indignant when it is suggested that they might be swayed by all this industry largesse. But why else would drug companies put so much money into them? As Stephen Goldfinger, chairman of the [American Psychology Association's] Committee on Commercial Support, said, "The pharmaceutical companies are an amoral bunch. They're not a benevolent association. So they are highly unlikely to donate large amounts of money without strings attached. Once one is dancing with the devil, you don't always get to call the steps of the dance."

Big pharma, for its part, insists that it has an educational mission that can be separated from its commercial interests. The 2002 PhRMA [Pharmaceutical Research and Manufacturers of America] Code on Interactions with Healthcare Professionals begins with the statement that "relationships with healthcare professionals ... should be focused on informing healthcare professionals about products, providing scientific and educational information, and supporting medical research and education." In other words, big pharma insists it is in the education business.

Gifts with a Research Purpose?

Then it goes on to recommend that companies not provide payments or gifts to doctors unless they serve an educational or research purpose. (Precisely how gifts serve such purposes is never explained.) In case there is any confusion, the code presents a series of hypothetical scenarios. Here are a couple:

> Question: Company A invites 300 physicians/consultants to a two-day and one-night speaker-training program at a regional golf resort. All attendees are compensated for their participation and their expenses are reimbursed. . . . Training sessions take both days, and the Company provides for a few hours of golf and meals. Does this program conform to the Code? . . .

Answer: This arrangement appears to comply with the Code. . . . [Spouses, it adds, should pay their own way.]

Question: Company A retains a small group of 15 nationally known physicians regarding a therapeutic area relevant to company A's products to advise on general medical and business issues and provide guidance on product development and research programs for those products. These physicians are paid significant fees, but those fees are typical of the fees paid to thought leaders in this therapeutic area. They normally meet once or twice a year at resort locations to discuss the latest product data, research programs and Company plans for the product(s). Does this comply with the Code? If it does, is it appropriate to pay for the spouse of the health care professional to attend, as well?

Answer: This arrangement appears to comply with the Code. . . . It would not be appropriate to pay for the cost of the spouse of the advisor.

You can see from these examples how calling marketing "education" and doctors "consultants" enables drug companies to evade antikickback laws. They can lay on all the boondoggles they want. . . .

It Takes Two

The pretense that pharmaceutical marketing is education requires the participation of at least two parties—the industry and the medical profession. We know why big pharma fosters that illusion: It helps the bottom line. It increases sales and promotes a highly drug-intensive style of medical practice. Indeed, if it didn't help the bottom line, if all this "education" were just that and had no impact on sales, heads would roll in the executive suites of the drug companies. After all, they are investor-owned businesses, and it is their responsibility to maximize profits, not give away billions of dollars.

It is much harder to excuse the medical profession and its institutions and organizations. Medical education worthy of the name requires an impartial analysis of all the available evidence, led by experts who have no vested interest in the drugs they are discussing. It is the job of medical schools and their faculty, and of professional societies, to educate doctors in that way. To abdicate that responsibility is wrong, and it is doubly wrong to leave it to an industry with an obvious financial interest in the enterprise and then pretend it is otherwise. That a noble profession has been willing to do this is a testament to the power of "food, flattery, and friendship"—and money, lots of it.

No one outside the industry has ever added up the costs of the "educational" activities described [here,] because they are not publicly disclosed. But these and similar activities could easily account for most of the unaccounted-for expenditures in big pharma's marketing budgets. It is far too much money to imagine that it represents some sort of public-spirited contribution to education. This masquerade leads to no end of problems—the corruption of the profession, the misuse and overuse of expensive prescription drugs, and . . . an avalanche of governmental investigations and lawsuits based on the spurious notion that the pharmaceutical industry provides bona fide medical education and it is therefore possible to distinguish lawful educational expenses from illegal marketing.

Periodical Bibliography

The following articles have been selected to supplement the diverse views presented in this chapter.

Paul Antony — Testimony to U.S. Senate Special Committee on Aging, September 29, 2005.

Troyen A. Brennan et al. — "Health Industry Practices That Create Conflicts of Interest," *Journal of the American Medical Association*, January 25, 2006.

Jay Cohen — "The Medical Profession's Culture of Corruption, Part 1," *MedicationSense*, January–April 2006. www.medicationsense.com.

Mark Crislip — "A Foolish Consistency," February 28, 2008. www.sciencebasedmedicine.org.

Michael D. Jibson — "Medical Education and the Pharmaceutical Industry: Managing an Uneasy Alliance," *Academic Psychiatry*, February 2006.

Jim Lehrer — Hosting *PBS Online NewsHour*, "Lipitor TV Spots Raise Debate over Advertising Practices," February 7, 2008. www.pbs.org.

Sally C. Pipes — "Drug Ads: Kill the Messenger?" *New York Post*, December 19, 2006.

Kurt C. Stange — "Time to Ban Direct-to-Consumer Prescription Drug Marketing," *Annals of Family Medicine*, March–April 2007.

Thomas P. Stossel — "Has the Hunt for Conflicts of Interest Gone Too Far? Yes," *British Medical Journal*, March 1, 2008.

Barbalee Symm et al. — "Effects of Using Free Sample Medications on the Prescribing Practices of Family Physicians," *Journal of the American Board of Family Medicine*, October 2006.

CHAPTER 4

Is the Cost of Prescription Drugs in America Appropriate?

Chapter Preface

More than 25 million people with AIDS have died since 1981. One doctor in South Africa, where nearly one thousand AIDS patients perish each day, says that hospitals short on drugs encourage patients to simply go home and die. President George W. Bush highlighted this advice in his 2003 State of the Union address: "In an age of miraculous medicines, no person should have to hear those words."

However, the cost of antiretroviral medicines, which slow the progression of the HIV virus that causes AIDS, is out of some people's reach. *The 12th Annual HIV Drug Guide* lists prices of HIV drugs in the United States: Crixivan is $548.12, Retrovir is $432.88, and the injectable drug Fuzeon for patients who have not benefited from other treatments runs $2,333.93—*per month*. For patients who are uninsured or underinsured, these high costs may mean going without medication. Consequently, some blame the pharmaceutical industry for charging high prices for antiretroviral drugs. Drug developers, responding to this claim, point to the many patients whose lives have improved or have been saved with medication, and contend that prices are justified.

U.S. pharmaceutical companies assert that they invest more time and money on drug research and development (R&D) than on any other entities. According to policy analyst Doug Bandow, "The $30,000,000,000 spent annually by U.S. drugmakers dwarfs the budget of the National Institutes of Health and investments by foreign drug companies." Their efforts result in life-saving medicines. Frank R. Lichtenberg's study in *Economics and Human Biology* estimates that over six thousand lives are saved per year with each HIV drug that is approved. He attributes the large drop in HIV deaths (12 percent from 1995–1996, according to the Centers for Disease Control and Prevention) to the HIV medicines introduced at that time. But finding one compound that completes all phases of clinical trials can cost as much as $800 million, claims drug industry representative Sidney Taurel. He testifies that when potential medicines fail clinical testing (as many do), the drug industry must recoup the money invested in their research. Heather Mason explains why her company, Abbott Laboratories, raised the price of its HIV drug Norvir in 2003: "We carefully considered many things, and ultimately . . . reach[ed] this difficult conclusion that this new price is necessary to be able to support our ability to continue research to bring the next generation of HIV medications to market." Besides, industry supporters point out, discounts are offered to patients who cannot afford antiretroviral drugs.

Unfortunately, it seems not everyone who needs help paying for drugs gets it. Patient advocates charge that the AIDS Drug Assistance Program (ADAP), meant to help hundreds of thousands of low-income people with HIV, is underfunded. Over six hundred people were denied drug coverage through the program in 2003, and at least ten patients in three states died while on the program's waiting list. In consequence, protestors are demanding that drug developers charge more affordable prices. The pharmaceutical industry's detractors also dispute the claim that the price of a drug is based on its cost of research and development. They recall that in 2003, Abbott raised the price of Norvir by five times when the drug had been on the market since 1996. From this, Clint Trout of the AIDS Healthcare Foundation surmises that "R&D really doesn't have that much influence on the price. . . . There is absolutely no reason but corporate greed for the Norvir price increase." Many critics suspect that the company raised rates to force patients to switch to Kaletra, its more expensive combination drug that contains Norvir.

Because so many things factor into the final cost of drugs, it is often difficult to evaluate the propriety of their prices. This evaluation is but one challenge faced by the analysts in the following chapter, as they deliberate whether drug prices are justified and whether laws are needed to help harness the cost of drugs.

> "Research pharmaceutical firms . . .
> must recover their huge front-end costs,
> which can run over $1 billion for a new
> drug."

The Cost of Prescription Drugs Is Justified

Richard A. Epstein

Richard A. Epstein is a senior fellow at the Hoover Institution, a think tank that promotes a free society, and author of Overdose: How Excessive Government Regulation Stifles Pharmaceutical Innovation. *In the following viewpoint, he insists that pharmaceutical prices are reasonable considering the immense cost of drug research and development. Costs are increasing because the FDA has added more barriers to drug approval, Epstein explains. Costs are further compounded by thousands of lawsuits against the pharmaceutical industry and by the expiration of successful drugs' patents, he maintains. Loss of drug company revenue, in Epstein's contention, hurts consumers because that means less money for the development of new medicines.*

As you read, consider the following questions:

1. How are pharmaceutical companies caught in a two-way vise, as Epstein explains it?
2. In the author's opinion, why are doctors afraid to prescribe drugs with black-box warnings?
3. How does the author respond to claims that marketing raises the cost of drugs?

The winds of political fortune have brought the Democrats into power in both houses of Congress, and high on their 2007 agenda is tightening the regulatory screws on the pharmaceutical industry. It seems highly likely that the new Congress will seek to intervene on such hot-button issues as FDA [Food and Drug Administration] oversight of drug safety, patent protection, and drug pricing.

The implicit premise behind this looming regulatory offensive is that Big Pharma (an epithet) is a 900-pound gorilla in need of domestication. In recent years, notable authors such as Arnold Relman, Marcia Angell, and Jerome Kassirer—all former editors in chief of the *New England Journal of Medicine*—have penned searing indictments of the industry.

These and other critics treat the industry's multibillion dollar profits as a sure sign of its permanent robust economic status. But those numbers conceal deep vulnerabilities. It is no accident that the shares of major pharmaceutical houses have been hammered [since 2003], even as profits appear to be at record highs. Wall Street values companies not only on current earnings, but also on long-term prospects, which are cloudy at best for research pharmaceutical firms. Just this past week [in November 2006], for example, Pfizer announced plans to cut one-fifth of its United States sales force, with a promise of further restructuring in January.

Pharmaceuticals Are Not Tobacco

We shouldn't be surprised. The huge profits of major drug firms are often tied to one or two drugs, such as Pfizer's Lipitor or Viagra—profits that evaporate when their patents expire and generics enter the marketplace. The Standard & Poor's review of pharmaceuticals thus starts somberly, noting that products with $21 billion in U.S. drug sales are going off patent in 2006, with another $24 billion to follow over the next three years—a sharp dent for an industry that today generates about $250 billion in revenue. All the while, the pharmaceutical houses also must absorb the legal and business risks needed to identify, patent, test, license, and market any new drug.

These trends should worry us all. Pharmaceuticals are not tobacco. There is no reason to rejoice in putting pharma on the ropes if its business reversals hurt the very consumers they are trying to serve. The medical advances of the past 30 years are not just a matter of dumb luck. They are very heavily dependent on the patent law, pricing freedom, and marketing strategies that have allowed these firms to bring a wide variety of vital products to market.

The champions of further regulation argue that their efforts won't limit innovations or curtail the widespread use of new drugs. But there are no free fixes. Too often ill-designed regulation gives us the worst of both worlds—slower innovation and more limited drug use.

The Trials and Tribulations of New Drug Development

We have much to fear in any new round of regulation. Bringing a new drug to market is already an arduous task. The FDA has consistently upped the number and type of clinical trials for companies seeking approval of new drugs, so that today as many as 60 separate trials are often required. Fewer drugs make it through these hurdles, and those that survive the ordeal cost ever more to bring to market.

Firms are thus caught in a two-way vise. They have to spend more to reach the market, yet once there they have a shorter period of patent exclusivity in which to recover their extensive front-end costs. (One consequence is that it has become ever harder to persuade companies to invest in drugs that attack diseases or conditions that afflict small populations—thus exposing companies to the charge that they heartlessly put profits before patient health.)

The risks of marketing a new drug have been further compounded as the FDA has become more willing to remove drugs from markets at the first sign of any real or imagined dangerous side effects. But while such FDA actions often lead to accusations that drug companies have not come clean about a product's risks, it is usually the FDA that makes the incorrect risk calculation.

[In 2005,] for example, early clinical trials showed great promise for a cancer drug called Iressa, which was used with success by many patients. After the early successes were not replicated in further clinical studies, the FDA adopted a Solomon-like solution: It allowed current users to continue receiving the drug, but otherwise took it off the market. The FDA's rationale was that a new drug, Tarceva, worked better. Yet it could never explain why patients for whom all other therapies had failed should prefer one last-ditch option to two. What is needed is good information about Iressa's successes and failures. If that is supplied, surely oncologists can do a better job calculating the odds than the FDA, which has to deal with averages, not individual cases.

Lawsuits Are Becoming Common

With other established drugs, like the antidepressants Zoloft and Prozac, the FDA leaves them on the market, but requires they be sold with severe "black-box" warnings that overstate the risks (in the case of Zoloft and Prozac, of suicide). Fearful physicians thus shy away from prescribing such drugs—not

Prescription Drugs Play a Pivotal Role in Improving Health Care and Reducing Medical Costs

Significant underdiagnosis and undertreatment of serious diseases is a growing health care problem in America. Americans would be healthier—and overall health care costs might actually decrease—if more patients were properly diagnosed and treated.

Prescription medicines play an important and growing role in basic health care. They are helping patients remain independent and productive. For example, the need for more expensive health care services such as long hospitalizations and surgeries can be reduced by using prescription medicines.

Currently, prescription drug expenditures account for less than 11 cents of every health care dollar. The good news is that while that percentage has increased in recent years, this increase means that more people are benefiting from more and better medicines. In fact, a study by Columbia University economist Frank Lichtenberg found that while treating conditions with newer medicines instead of older ones increases medicine costs, it significantly lowers non-drug medical spending. The study found that each additional dollar spent on using a newer prescription medicine (instead of an older one) saves roughly $7.20 in other health care costs.

Pharmaceutical Research and Manufacturers of America,
What Goes into the Cost of Prescription Drugs?
June 2005. www.phrma.org/files/Cost_of_Prescription_Drugs.pdf.

because of the dangers the drugs pose, but because they fear the warnings expose them to greater risk of medical malpractice suits.

Pharmaceutical companies meanwhile have their own lawsuits to worry about. The liability risks of mass-marketed drugs have increased significantly in recent years. Consumer fraud class actions, now common, arise after drugs have been withdrawn for some adverse side effect. Nonetheless, litigants are often allowed to sue for refunds not only for unused drugs, but also for the drugs that were successfully used, on the grounds that if the truth about the side effects had not been concealed (itself a debatable proposition), the pills would never have been purchased in the first place. The resulting loss in revenue leaves drug companies with even fewer resources to cover the thousands of suits for compensatory and punitive damages for drug-related injuries, like the multiple suits brought against Merck for its drug Vioxx.

Personal injury claims are immensely expensive to defend individually and their outcomes are fraught with error. Often they are propelled by inflammatory trial techniques that obscure the scientific evidence, which lay juries find hard to assess in the first place. It is stark evidence of how dire the situation is for pharmaceutical companies that the FDA, typically no friend of the drug companies on safety issues, has now actively intervened on their side in personal injury suits that attack the adequacy of FDA-approved warnings.

The common judicial refrain in tort litigation has long been that FDA oversight, no matter how comprehensive, supplies only a "minimum" set of warnings. In reality, however, excessive warning is the greater peril. The FDA faces fierce criticism from Congress, the medical profession, and the popular press whenever any approved drug exhibits adverse side effects. Yet these watchdogs offer little or no outcry when the FDA keeps a new drug off the market. Visible injuries are easier to track than lost opportunities for cure.

Drug Profits Pay for Future Medical Advances

Perhaps the biggest threat on the horizon for the drug industry is mounting pressure to submit to price controls. One possibility is that the government will set uniform prices for all drugs. Another is that it would require a company to sell to all customers at the lowest price charged to any customer within the past year. But no matter how such controls are calculated, they could devastate the business. What's more, they're just not necessary.

Traditionally, patent holders could decide how much to charge for their wares. Public protection against excessive profits for drug companies came from three sources. First, the patent period is limited to 20 years, with about half that time used to shepherd a new drug through the FDA approval process. Once the patent expires, the entry of low-cost generics sharply reduces the cost of proven drugs. Second, the rapid pace of invention means that consumers frequently can choose between two or more patented drugs in the same class (Lipitor, Crestor, and Zocor, for example, are three statins used to lower cholesterol), effectively blunting the monopoly power of all patent holders. Third, antitrust laws make it illegal for any makers of the same or similar drugs to conspire to raise prices or reduce output.

Within these constraints, of course, the research pharmaceutical firms still must recover their huge front-end costs, which can run over $1 billion for a new drug, over an ever shorter useful patent life. In addition, their successful drugs must generate additional revenues to cover the predictable flops. Yet companies need to charge someone for the initial costs of production, not just for the small cost of producing additional pills.

One common argument for price controls is that drug companies should only spend money for research but not for lavish marketing. Yet that short-sighted argument assumes that pharmaceutical companies could sell the same quantities of drugs without advertising them. Of course, the cost of marketing raises the total cost of production, but by expanding the consumer base, it lowers the average costs consumers pay per unit. Any system of direct price controls would thus play havoc with both research and marketing, drying up the capital needed for innovation.

The overall picture today shows a research drug industry under constant pressure from all sides. Industry critics greatly fear letting bad drugs on the market, while simultaneously underestimating the real costs (in the form of forgone health benefits) of keeping good drugs off the market. In reality any sound risk assessment, whether by regulation or litigation, should take into account both kinds of error.

Critics also naively assume that investors and firms will continue to make huge investments in new products without any assurance of recouping their costs in the marketplace. But the drug business is too vast and complex to depend on individual altruism or government bureaucrats to fuel medical advances. As [economist] Adam Smith recognized long ago, the profit motive is the only constant and reliable spur to making the major investments on which the prosperity (and health) of any nation depends. Today's pharmaceutical industry is not exempt from that enduring insight.

"Price gouging by the pharmaceutical industry is allowing industry profits to soar at the expense of every American."

The Cost of Prescription Drugs Is Outrageous

Alliance for Retired Americans Educational Fund

In the following viewpoint, Alliance for Retired Americans Educational Fund blasts drug manufacturers for charging prices that it claims are unjustifiably high—and still growing. The pharmaceutical industry blocks efforts to loosen its hold on high drug prices, the alliance asserts. Drugmakers exaggerate the cost of developing new medicines and absorb their exorbitant marketing costs into drug prices, according to the alliance. Furthermore, it contends that manufacturers charge different people different prices for drugs, leaving those without insurance to pay the most. Alliance for Retired Americans Educational Fund conducts research to help advance public policy that preserves the health and economic security of seniors.

As you read, consider the following questions:

1. What is the true cost of research and development of a new drug, according to an independent estimate cited by the alliance?

Diane M. Porter, *Outrageous Fortune: How the Drug Industry Profits from Pills*, Washington, DC: Alliance for Retired Americans Educational Fund, August 2007. Reprinted with permission of the Alliance for Retired Americans Educational Fund.

2. How many pharmaceutical sales representatives does America have, in the author's assertion?

3. What does the alliance say is resulting from the "quicker and sicker" discharge of patients from hospitals?

The volume and expenditure for drugs sold has increased dramatically in recent years. Between 1994 and 2005, the number of prescription drugs purchased has increased 71 percent—from 2.1 billion to 3.6 billion—compared to a U.S. population growth of 9 percent. The U.S. Department of Health and Human Services projects national prescription drug spending will increase 148 percent from 2005–2016.

Despite the claims of supporters of the 2003 Medicare Modernization Act (MMA), the new drug benefit provided by private insurers has not reduced prescription drug prices for Medicare beneficiaries or the program. Overall, it is projected that Medicare beneficiaries will spend $1.2 trillion on prescription drugs over the next decade. Since the MMA took effect, Medicare is now the largest public payer of prescription drugs with Medicare spending rising to 22 percent of total U.S. prescription spending in 2006, up from 2 percent in 2005.

It is extremely difficult to identify the actual cost of a drug because the pricing chains are complex. Variations in the price take place because of the power the drug companies have in their market. Drug manufacturers charge different customers different prices for the same drug as large purchasers can obtain discounts and rebates. At the bottom of the pricing chain, it is the individual consumer without insurance coverage who pays the highest prices for prescription drugs.

Refuting Pharmaceutical Companies' Claims About Drug Costs

The pharmaceutical industry claims that the high prices of new drugs are necessary to fund ongoing research and development (R&D) maintaining that it costs $800 million to develop a new drug. However, an independent estimate places the R&D costs for a new drug at half the industry's claim. Most core research for drugs is actually funded by the federal government, primarily through the National Institutes of Health and universities. Moreover, much of the drug manufacturers' development of drugs is not for new drugs but rather copies of existing drugs.

Drug manufacturers also claim that drug prices must be higher in the United States because price controls in other developed countries do not pay sufficiently for R&D costs. Yet, European countries develop many innovative new drugs in the world market accounting for 36 percent of total R&D spending, 32 percent of new molecular entities, and 28 percent of world sales.

How Drug Marketing Factors In

Pharmaceutical companies benefit from many tax deductions, tax credits and tax havens. Many enjoy greater profits as a percent of revenue than companies in other industries, even beating the three top-ranked companies in the *Fortune* 500 list. In 2005, the seven pharmaceutical companies with the highest revenues [declared more of their revenue as profits than the percentage spent on] research and development— and [spent] even more on marketing. More than 17 percent of their revenues were dedicated to profits, compared with 13.9 percent spent on R&D and 32 percent on marketing, advertising and administration.

A significant amount of prescription drug money goes straight to the chief executive officers (CEOs) of drug companies with most of them receiving total compensation packages of millions of dollars.

Drug manufacturers promote the use of new or altered drugs primarily through contacts with physicians and direct-to-consumer advertising (DTCA). The pharmaceutical industry employs 100,000 drug representatives or 2.5 for every

Same Drugs, Higher Prices

It is now widely known that a given prescription can cost an American patient more than twice what the same drug made by the same company will cost a patient in Canada, England, or most of continental Europe. The Organisation for Economic Co-operation and Development [OECD] is a multinational consortium that tracks data on economic activity in about 30 nations. A recent OECD report compared drug expenditures in 14 advanced industrial countries. The average amount spent per capita on medications in the United States was 65 percent higher than the average per capita drug expenditure in the rest of these nations, all of which have highly developed economies. . . .

We Americans are often perversely proud of how much we spend on things, perhaps assuming that if we pay a lot for a product or service it must be of high quality. (As [historian] Barbara Tuchman noted, this helps explain the popularity of powdered pearls as a treatment for the Black Plague.) But a systematic survey of patients in five English-speaking countries doesn't confirm the idea that spending more has made Americans more content about their prescription drugs. The U.S. citizens took more medications than respondents in Australia, Canada, the United Kingdom, and New Zealand, but they also reported the highest rates of side effects, of skipping doses to make a prescription last longer, and of not being able to fill a prescription at all because of its cost. (This last problem was reported by one in three American patients; an earlier survey found that the rate was one in two for Americans with incomes below the national average, if they lacked health insurance.)

Jerry Avorn, Powerful Medicines.
New York: Alfred A. Knopf, 2004.

practicing doctor in the country. Marketing directed toward doctors in 2005 amounted to $7.2 billion and often includes meals and gifts. This does not include the retail value of samples left at doctors' offices, which totaled $16 billion. Since 1997, DCTA has become a more significant part of marketing amounting to $4.8 billion in 2006, a 13 percent increase over 2005 and five times the amount spent in 1996. Drug companies also spend millions in contributions to political candidates and to lobby Congress and state legislators.

Today, generics represent 63 percent of the total prescriptions dispensed in the United States, but less than 20 percent of all dollars spent on prescription drugs indicating how far less costly generic drugs are. Generic drugs are able to enter the market only after the brand-name company's patent expires. However, generic entry can be delayed when patents are extended by various means, including settlements with generic companies.

Ultimately, the best and most comprehensive approach to providing affordable prescription drugs for all the American people is to create a high quality, affordable, universal health care system, which provides comprehensive services and is based on a sound financing model similar to Medicare.

The Enhancement of Life Comes at Great Cost

Toward the end of the 20th century, changes were made in the way hospitals were compensated that prompted them to reduce the length of stay of patients. This "quicker and sicker" discharge from hospitals led physicians to increasingly rely on prescription drugs for treating patients. There is no doubt the introduction of many new drugs has extended and enhanced the quality of everyday life for millions of Americans. Technological advances in treating diseases include the utilization of new drugs that can arrest or cure many cancers, heart disease, high blood pressure, AIDS and other life-threatening conditions.

Drug interventions forestall the hospitalization of many other older persons and help them to maintain lives outside of institutions. Consequently, the role prescription drugs play in the lives of older persons, in particular, has become much greater. However, although drugs have contributed to reducing costs associated with hospitalizations and surgeries, new drugs are more expensive than older drugs, and three times more costly than generic drugs.

In May 2001, the Alliance for Retired Americans released its inaugural report, *The Profit in Pills: A Primer on Prescription Drug Prices*, to make the public aware of how price gouging by the pharmaceutical industry is allowing industry profits to soar at the expense of every American and every U.S. company providing health benefits. Since then, a number of books, news articles and other reports have exposed the extent and means by which the pharmaceutical industry protects its hold on high drug prices and profits. . . .

There have not been any improvements to prescription drug access nor lowering of drug costs. Rather, the pharmaceutical industry continues to exert wide-ranging influence in various areas to protect its profits and forestall attempts to lower prices. The launch of a flawed Medicare prescription drug benefit in 2006 has been a particular windfall for drug manufacturers with expanded prescription drug sales but without an accompanying reduction in prices for beneficiaries.

The Price of Prescription Drugs Is Escalating

- Expenditures for prescription drugs were $200.7 billion in 2005, five times the $40.3 billion spent in 1990.

- The U.S. Department of Health and Human Services projects national prescription drug spending will increase 148 percent from 2005–2016.

- Eighty-nine percent of new drugs in the U.S. offer little or no additional benefit over existing drugs, yet U.S. drug prices are the highest in the world.

- In 2006, the first year of the Medicare prescription drug benefit, U.S. medication sales increased by $2.5 billion with the Medicare benefit accounting for one-sixth of the total increase in sales.

- There are hidden prices, discounts and rebates for different purchasers. The pricing chain for drugs is complex and difficult to trace because the drug industry considers much of the information proprietary and hence is not publicly available.

> *"Through cooperative governmental efforts, we drink imported fruit juice and eat imported meats with confidence. We can accomplish the same for prescription drugs."*

Americans Should Be Able to Buy Cheaper Drugs Outside the Country

Gil Gutknecht

Gil Gutknecht, author of the following viewpoint, is chairman of the House Agricultural Subcommittee on Department Operations, Oversight, Nutrition and Forestry; vice chairman of the House Science Committee; and a member of the House Budget Committee. Gutknecht endorses the importation of prescription drugs from foreign countries because, according to Gutknecht, Americans illegally purchase medications from other countries to save on costs, but have no protections against counterfeit or contaminated drugs. Therefore, Gutknecht encourages the government to legalize and regulate the importation of medications

Gil Gutknecht, "Q: Have Pharmaceutical Companies Been Unfair to American Consumers? Yes: Americans Should Not Have to Pay Significantly More for the Same Prescription Drugs as Our Friends in Canada and Europe (Symposium)," *Insight on the News*, August 19, 2003, p. 46. Copyright © 2003 News World Communications, Inc. All rights reserved. Reproduced with permission of Insight.

provided they are FDA-approved and made in plants inspected by the FDA. In his opinion, Americans deserve safe prescription drugs at the lowest prices possible.

As you read, consider the following questions:

1. The Pharmaceutical Market Access Act allows market access to FDA-approved pharmaceuticals from FDA-approved facilities in how many industrialized countries?
2. According to the viewpoint, Americans can pay how many times more for the same prescription drugs as their counterparts around the world?
3. Why did Gutknecht vote against the House prescription-drug benefit?

There is little question that increasing health care costs are a problem that affects all Americans. Small businesses have difficulty hiring new employees because they can't afford to provide health insurance. Seniors are forced to cut prescriptions in half or skip meals. Moms and dads struggle to meet the basic health care needs of their children. Prescription-drug prices continue to increase at four to five times the rate of inflation.

The Bush administration and congressional leadership, in an attempt to address some of these concerns, proposed a prescription-drug benefit under Medicare. . . . Several weeks ago [in Augist 2003] The House passed HR 1, the Prescription Drug and Medicare Modernization Act of 2003, by a razor-thin 216–215 vote. Unfortunately, this legislation does little to address the driver of increasing health care costs: exorbitant prescription-drug prices.

Making a Bad Situation Worse

I hope I'm wrong, but I am afraid the proposed benefit may only make a bad situation worse. With 40 million baby boomers set to retire in the next 20 years, a benefit that fails

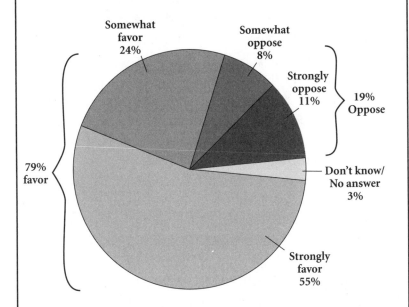

The Majority of Americans Support Buying Prescription Drugs from Canada

Do you favor or oppose Congress changing the law to allow Americans to buy prescription drugs from Canada at lower cost?

Somewhat favor 24%

Somewhat oppose 8%

Strongly oppose 11%

19% Oppose

79% favor

Don't know/ No answer 3%

Strongly favor 55%

TAKEN FROM: Kaiser Family Foundation/Harvard School of Public Health, *The Public's Health Care Agenda for the New Congress and Presidential Campaign*, December 2006.

to address the price side will result in staggering deficits, dramatic tax increases or both. If tax cuts are supposed to stimulate the economy today, what will be the effect of massive tax increases in coming years?

Fortunately, Congress has passed HR 2427, the Pharmaceutical Market Access Act, allowing market access to Food and Drug Administration (FDA) approved pharmaceuticals from FDA-approved facilities in 25 industrialized countries. This legislation had broad support in the House and had the support of real seniors groups across the country. I say "real" seniors groups to distinguish between groups composed of and funded by seniors and those created by the pharmaceutical industry.

One example of the latter is the Seniors Coalition of Springfield, Va. This organization sent thousands of mailings across the United States but, sadly, the Seniors Coalition is funded by the pharmaceutical industry to protect the industry's interests.

No one disputes that Americans pay as much as 10 times more for the same prescription drugs as our counterparts around the world. I have no problem helping our friends in sub-Saharan Africa, but I do have a problem with American consumers subsidizing the starving Swiss.

Patricia Reinartz of Austin, Minn., is a classic example. She is a senior who takes Protenix and Premarin. Reinartz was spending $360 per month to fill her prescriptions. She now imports these same FDA-approved drugs at a cost of $210 per month. Although $150 per month might not seem like much to a pharmaceutical executive, to seniors living on fixed incomes it can be the difference between despair and dignity. In Reinartz's own words, "Please keep working for prescription-drug importation. I order from abroad; it works great!"

Reinartz has decided to risk FDA prosecution in order to sustain her health. She shouldn't be branded a common criminal because Congress stands between her and the opportunity to purchase pharmaceuticals at world-market prices. If Reinartz can buy imported meat and vegetables from the local grocery store, shouldn't she be able to purchase her medication in a free market as well?

Kate Stahl is an 84-year-old grandmother who volunteers for the Minnesota Senior Federation. Stahl joined me on Capitol Hill when I introduced HR 2427. In the June 9 [2003] *U.S. News and World Report* she said, "I'd like nothing better than to be thrown in jail [for importing prescription drugs]." It's outrageous that she would even have to consider such drastic measures, but she is standing on the shoulders of patriots as she stands up for American seniors.

The Government Should Create Standards for Imported Drugs

For every other consumable good, Congress, the FDA and the U.S. Department of Agriculture (USDA) have created standards and regulations to promote safety in importation. Food products are imported in massive quantities. Through cooperative governmental efforts, we drink imported fruit juice and eat imported meats with confidence. We can accomplish the same for prescription drugs.

The FDA's concerns for safety apparently do not extend to seniors who cannot afford their prescribed drugs. Americans such as Reinartz and Stahl are crossing the border for cheaper drugs in order to sustain their health. But the FDA does not look at this issue as if they are sustaining their health. The FDA sees only that they are improperly importing pharmaceuticals. This is outrageous! As my good friend and pharmaceutical-market-access expert Steve Schondelmeyer of the University of Minnesota PRIME Institute says, "A drug you cannot afford is neither safe nor effective."

So true. On a recent trip to Germany, I purchased 10 of the most commonly prescribed drugs from the airport pharmacy in Munich for a total cost of $373.30. Those same drugs cost a whopping $1,039.65 in the United States.

These price disparities are not isolated to a few drugs. My 86-year-old father takes Coumadin, a commonly prescribed blood thinner. A 30-day supply of Coumadin costs $89.95 in the United States, but only $21 in Germany. Tamoxifen, a miracle breast-cancer drug that was developed almost entirely with American taxpayer dollars, costs $360 in the United States, but only $60 in Germany. This, unfortunately, is the rule rather than the exception.

For its part, GlaxoSmithKline, under the auspices of re-newed "safety concerns," is threatening to stop shipping its products to Canadian wholesalers and pharmacies that sell to American patients as of January 2003. Despite clinging to claims of the dangers of counterfeit and misbranded drugs, Glaxo has been unable to cite a single incident of damage caused by imported FDA-approved prescription drugs.

Pharmaceutical companies are urging U.S consumers to ignore the man behind the curtain. Facts are stubborn things. And the fact is that Americans pay significantly more for the same prescription drugs as our friends in Canada and Europe. At the same time, U.S. taxpayers are subsidizing the rest of the world by paying a lion's share of development costs.

The Safety Issue

The safety issue is a red herring. The real issue is the prices Americans pay and the effect they will have on any prescription-drug benefit.

According to the Congressional Budget Office, seniors alone will spend $1.8 trillion on prescription drugs during the next 10 years. Proponents of the prescription-drug benefit claim the cost will not exceed the $400 billion set aside. Does anyone believe we will solve a $1.8 trillion problem with a $400 billion solution?

The history of federal entitlements teaches that costs will escalate. For that matter, considering that it is an entitlement and has no fixed budget, does anyone believe it will cost less than $1.8 trillion? In fact, according to Texas A&M University's Social Security and Medicare Trustees/Private Enterprise Re-search Center, the new drug benefit will cost a whopping $7.5 trillion.

What's worse, included in the entitlement are the wealthy. In a time when we are facing record deficits, is it wise to pro-vide a prescription-drug benefit for Ross Perot? As my friend

Rep. John Shadegg (R-Ariz.) says, "To provide a generous universal subsidy to retirees regardless of how wealthy is bad public policy."

We simply cannot afford to pass a prescription-drug benefit without considering costs. Without competitive pressure, the giant pharmaceutical companies well may shift savings from any discounts given to Medicare onto the backs of businesses, the underinsured and the uninsured. One way to keep costs in check is to open markets.

Affordable Prescriptions for All Americans

Because the House prescription-drug benefit failed to address the outrageously high prices of prescription drugs, I voted against it. This is a matter of generational fairness for our kids and grandkids. And it's a matter of giving seniors real reform that provides affordable prescription drugs for all Americans.

Congress should refocus the FDA on its fundamental mission of protecting public health, as well as open the United States to modern, industrialized markets for FDA-approved prescription drugs from FDA-approved facilities. Americans depend on competitive prices provided by free markets. Congress should act immediately to open up those markets fully and completely.

Modern bar-coded technology, together with counterfeit-proof packaging, can ensure safety and quality. Open markets will ensure affordability. Americans deserve world-class prescription drugs at world-market prices.

> "Estimates of fatalities caused by coun-
> terfeit drugs run as high as 200,000
> worldwide."

Americans Should Not Be Permitted to Buy Drugs Outside the Country

Michelle Plasari

Allowing Americans to buy medications from foreign countries would spur an influx of counterfeit, expired, or otherwise unsafe drugs into the U.S., argues Michelle Plasari in the following viewpoint. Plasari details the problems faced by countries that have opened their borders to foreign drugs. A shocking number of medicines, she claims, are counterfeit or made in countries like China that, she says, produce substandard products. The FDA itself, she points out, admits it cannot guarantee the safety of imported drugs. Michelle Plasari is the president of RetireSafe, which works to protect the benefits and retirement of the elderly.

As you read, consider the following questions:

1. What concerns about drug importation does Plasari say politicians have forgotten?

2. What source cited by the author estimates that the sales of fake drugs will increase by more than 90 percent from 2005 to 2010?

3. From which countries did most of the 560,598 fake drugs seized by European Union customs come, in the author's assertion?

Recent events featuring dangerous Chinese imports of toxic lead-painted toys, tainted dog food, contaminated toothpaste, and other substandard consumer products have outraged consumers and led to congressional hearings on how to protect the public. The ghastly images of sick children and dying pets illustrate the frightening future we face if some in Congress get their way and hundreds of millions of foreign medications begin pouring into our nation.

Championing a Dangerous Cause

The distorted vision of mass prescription drug importation has become so attractive to politicians at every level that they are lining up to wave their legislative wands to make it happen. Once again, the House of Representatives seems poised to open our borders to allow our closed drug system to be breached. With cheap drugs as their battle cry, these elected panderers loudly vie to be the champions of importing huge amounts of foreign medications into the United States.

That's business as usual; politicians have always tested the wind to see what's popular (cheap drugs)—and then champion that cause. This time, they have failed to make the connection with recent events, and they have forgotten to answer some important concerns. What about the growing epidemic of counterfeit medications plaguing the rest of the world? What about the drug safety we expect and depend on? What will these same elected officials say when people die because of their policies? Who will stand up and take responsibility for the damage?

Both the U S. Food and Drug Administration (FDA) and the Secretary of Health and Human Services (HHS) have warned that if importation is allowed, we will be opening our borders to counterfeit drugs, cheap foreign copies of FDA-approved drugs, expired and/or contaminated drugs, and drugs stored or transported under unsafe conditions. The FDA has said repeatedly that it can not guarantee the safety of medicines coming into the U.S. from foreign countries.

Counterfeit Drugs Across the World

The numbers are staggering. The World Health Organization (WHO) has warned that up to "ten percent of medicines available globally are counterfeits, posing a serious health hazard." In one FDA and U.S. Customs Department investigation targeting imported prescription drugs entering our country, some 88 percent of the medicines discovered were found to be unapproved or otherwise illegal. The Center for Medicines in the Public Interest (based in the U.S.) projects counterfeit drug sales to reach $75 billion around the globe by 2010, a five-year increase of more than 90 percent. The WHO today estimates that "25 percent to 50 percent of the drugs consumed in developing countries are counterfeit."

The House importation legislation would allow drugs from Australia, Austria, Belgium, Bulgaria, Canada, Cyprus, Czech Republic, Denmark, Estonia, Finland, France, Germany, Greece, Hungary, Ireland, Italy, Japan, Latvia, Lithuania, Luxembourg, Malta, Netherlands, New Zealand, Portugal, Romania, Slovakia, Spain, Sweden, Switzerland, and the United Kingdom. Most of these countries are the same European Union (EU) countries now fighting a growing problem of counterfeit drugs resulting from their "parallel trade" policy [which allows drug importation from other countries].

A report by the Council of Europe found that, "The existence of a significant level of parallel trade in the EU, in the absence of adequate controls of repackaging and relabeling, provides an opportunity for the inadvertent entry of counterfeit drugs into the market. . . . Furthermore, parallel trade means that any counterfeit drug within the legitimate distribution chain in one Member State can easily contaminate other Member States." In that regard, EU customs seizures published in November 2006 recorded more than 560,598 packets of fake medicine seized last year. The large majority came from India, Egypt, and China. What a great place for Americans to get their medicines!

Deaths tolls are rising from fake medications around the world. Estimates of fatalities caused by counterfeit drugs run as high as 200,000 worldwide, according to the WHO. These deaths include people in British Columbia and the U.S. who purchased drugs at supposed Canadian pharmacies. Few medicines are produced in Canada, and studies have shown that many of the drugs alleged to be from Canada were actually imported to Canada from countries like Pakistan, Brazil, Bangladesh, China, South Africa, and even Saudi Arabia and Iran. That's why the FDA has repeatedly opposed drug importation from Canada. As scary as it may be—Canada may be the safest country listed in the House importation bill. Happy Halloween! This bill could be quite a fatal trick.

For those reasons, this dangerous drug importation measure must be defeated. Hopefully the adults in Congress will defeat it, or the president will veto it before all Americans, and especially seniors and children, are put at risk.

> *"The federal government and Medicare beneficiaries would save $600 billion between 2006 and 2013 if Medicare were allowed ... to negotiate prices."*

The Government Should Allow Price Negotiations for Medicare Drugs

National Committee to Preserve Social Security and Medicare

In the following viewpoint, the National Committee to Preserve Social Security and Medicare (NCPSSM) contends that drug costs could be lowered by letting the Medicare program negotiate prices with pharmaceutical companies. Federally negotiated medication prices, like those achieved by the Department of Veterans Affairs, come at substantial discounts, according to NCPSSM. In the committee's estimation, Medicare beneficiaries would save billions of dollars if it adopted similar negotiations. NCPSSM is a nonpartisan, nonprofit organization that aims to create a secure retirement for Americans.

National Committee to Preserve Social Security and Medicare, "Price Negotiation Would Dramatically Lower the Cost of Prescription Drugs for Medicare Beneficiaries," April 2006. www.ncpssm.org. Reproduced with permission.

As you read, consider the following questions:

1. How many beneficiaries does Medicare have, according to NCPSSM?
2. In the author's contention, what government agencies get Federal Supply Schedule prices?
3. How much higher are average prices of the ten leading private Medicare drug plans than federally negotiated prices, in NCPSSM's assertion?

The National Committee to Preserve Social Security and Medicare (NCPSSM) has long advocated for a government-administered [Medicare] Part D benefit with negotiated drug prices. However, a provision in the Medicare Modernization Act (MMA), known as the "noninterference" provision, expressly prohibits the Medicare program from directly negotiating lower prescription drug prices with pharmaceutical manufacturers. Over 3,000 private plans enter into negotiations with pharmaceutical manufacturers to deliver Medicare Part D benefits. Each plan tries to attract a large enough number of customers so they have more leverage to negotiate lower prices with manufacturers. Establishing Medicare as the collective buyer of prescription drugs—rather than thousands of individual private plans—would better harness the purchasing power of Medicare's 43 million beneficiaries and substantially lower prices.

Medicare Prices Are Much Higher than Federally Negotiated Drug Prices

The National Committee is committed to finding ways to improve the prescription drug law. One of the most significant improvements we can make is to allow the traditional Medicare program to offer its own government-administered Part D plan with drug prices negotiated directly with pharmaceutical manufacturers.

A Medical Professor Advocates Medicare Drug Price Negotiations

The idea that Medicare would name the price it is willing to pay for something is not entirely foreign. Medicare already dictates doctors' fees and laboratory and hospital reimbursement. Under the current system, doctors have an option. We can be Medicare providers and accept that the prices the government decides are fair and reasonable, or we can go outside the system entirely and not accept Medicare at all. If we choose the latter, our elderly patients will not be reimbursed for our services. We can charge top dollar, but then many patients would not be able to come to us. We will survive outside the system if we provide an exclusive service that is in high demand.... The same logic would apply to drug manufacturers.

Marc Siegel,
"This Doesn't Have To Be the Price We Pay,"
Washington Post, *June 22, 2003.*

Medicare beneficiaries deserve the same low prices that veterans and others receive through negotiations between the federal government and drug companies. The Department of Veterans Affairs (VA) achieves significant discounts on generic and brand-name prescription drugs by negotiating directly with pharmaceutical manufacturers on behalf of its five million beneficiaries. One study by Congressional Budget Office (CBO) found that, on average, the VA pays only about 42% of the Average Wholesale Price (AWP)—or the suggested list price—for brand-name drugs.

While VA beneficiaries enjoy some of the best prices on prescription drugs negotiated by the federal government, other federal departments also receive significant discounts on prescription drugs through price negotiation. For example, CBO found that drug prices negotiated through the Federal Supply Schedule (FSS) are 53% of the AWP. FSS prices are available to all government agencies (including the VA, the Department of Defense, the Public Health Service, the Bureau of Prisons, and other federal agencies and institutions) when they purchase prescription drugs.

Seniors pay more for prescription drugs under Medicare Part D than veterans pay for prescription drugs under their federally-negotiated plan. One study by Families USA found that the VA negotiated substantially lower prices for the top 20 drugs used by seniors, compared to private Medicare Part D plans. Specifically, they found that the lowest VA price is lower than the lowest Medicare prescription drug plan price for 19 of the top 20 drugs. Based on an analysis of median prices, Families USA also found that the lowest price offered by any Medicare prescription drug plan is at least $260.70, or 48.2%, higher than the lowest price available through the VA.

Another study by the minority staff at the House Government Reform Committee found that drug prices under Medicare Part D's private plans exceed federally-negotiated prices, Canadian prices, Drugstore.com prices, and Costco prices. Their study showed that the average prices offered by the ten leading private Medicare drug plans are 84% higher than federally negotiated prices (Federal Supply Schedule), 61% higher than Canadian prices, 3.5% higher than Drugstore.com prices, and 2.9% higher than Costco prices.

What Would Be the Effect on Drug Costs?

A Medicare-operated Part D plan with drug prices directly negotiated with pharmaceutical companies will deliver billions of dollars in savings. Research by respected economist Dean Baker shows that the federal government and Medicare beneficiaries would save $600 billion between 2006 and 2013 if Medicare were allowed to directly offer a Part D benefit and to negotiate prices with pharmaceutical manufacturers. Such significant savings could be used to close Part D's donut hole [its coverage gap in which beneficiaries pay the total cost of their drugs] and to lower cost-sharing for Medicare beneficiaries.

Medicare beneficiaries should be given the choice to get their prescription drug benefit from the traditional Medicare program that they know and trust. Instead, they are forced to deal with an overwhelming number of private plans with varying formularies, premiums, deductibles, and co-pays in order to receive prescription drug coverage. A Medicare-operated plan with negotiated drug prices will restore the social insurance nature of Medicare, deliver substantially lower prices, and give beneficiaries the Part D choice they really want.

"Almost 200 new drugs would go undiscovered over the next two decades as an indirect result of federal price negotiations."

The Government Should Not Allow Price Negotiations for Medicare Drugs

Benjamin Zycher

Benjamin Zycher, a senior fellow at the Manhattan Institute Center for Medical Progress, contends in the following viewpoint that permitting price negotiations for Medicare drugs would harm pharmaceutical research and development. Should the government allow such negotiations, he explains, pharmaceutical companies would lose revenue. With less money to invest in research and development of new medicines, health care would suffer, predicts Zycher. He compares the Medicare drug negotiation proposal to the Department of Veterans Affairs' drug program, which he claims offers fewer choices and covers only older, cheaper, less effective medications.

Benjamin Zycher, "The Human Cost of Drug Price Negotiations," *Real Clear Politics*, November 29, 2006. Reproduced by permission.

As you read, consider the following questions:

1. How many drugs are on the VA (Veterans Affairs) formulary compared to Medicare's formularies, according to Zycher?

2. In the author's view, how do the incentives of government negotiators differ from those of private firms?

3. How many years of life does Zycher predict would be lost if Medicare price negotiations are allowed?

Lowering prices for prescription drugs for the elderly is a politically attractive idea. So, it is hardly surprising that incoming House Speaker Nancy Pelosi has announced that in the first 100 hours of the new Congress she will seek to empower the federal government to negotiate drug prices directly with pharmaceutical companies providing medicines for the new Medicare prescription drug benefit. She believes, with good reason, that the massive size and buying power of the federal government would drive those prices down to unprecedented levels.

She is right that prices would come down, but she is wrong that using the power of the federal government would come without a high cost: a reduction in the creation of new and improved medicines that would lessen future human suffering. The development of fewer new medicines would be the collateral damage inflicted by government negotiations that would lower industry returns and reduce R&D [research and development] spending. My own estimate, based on existing government data, would be that almost 200 new drugs would go undiscovered over the next two decades as an indirect result of federal price negotiations.

A Look at the VA's Price-Negotiated Program

To understand why this is true, it is instructive to review the actual experience of the drug purchasing program adminis-

In Opposition of Fixed Prices for Medicare Drugs

Price controls would have serious consequences for patients. If only lower priced and less effective drug alternatives are available, costs will rise due to over-utilization of drugs on the market and added physician and hospital visits. If Congress ultimately requires companies to stay at the table and "negotiate," drug prices would likely rise higher than the current equilibrium price for other consumers, because companies would cost-shift and raise wholesale prices to moderate their anticipated losses. In either scenario, government intrusion into the pharmaceutical marketplace would significantly deter private sector innovation and produce vast, incalculable costs by inhibiting medical progress and undermining decisions regarding clinical appropriateness that had previously been made by patients and doctors.

Greg D'Angelo,
"Why the New Congress Should Not Fix Drug Prices,"
Heritage Foundation WebMemo,
December 1, 2006. www.heritage.org.

tered by the Department of Veterans Affairs [VA] cited by many as a "negotiating" model for Medicare Part D. In order to reduce budget costs, the VA excludes newer and more expensive medicines. The VA "formulary," a list of covered medicines, includes about 1400 drugs; virtually all of the existing Part D formularies, currently negotiated by private purchasers, have about 4300 drugs.

What is more striking is that drugs covered by the VA formulary are significantly older than those covered by Medicare Part D or by private health insurance plans. The VA formulary includes only 38 percent of the drugs approved by the FDA during the 1990s, only 19 percent of the drugs approved since 2000, and only 22 percent of the drugs given priority review approval since 1997. VA prescriptions systematically are for drugs older than those specified in non-VA prescriptions, and new drugs as a matter of VA policy are not considered for the VA formulary for three years, regardless of improved effectiveness or reduced side effects. A third of VA seniors prefer to switch to Part D, but cannot because they would lose other VA benefits.

Government negotiators—at the VA and elsewhere—have very different incentives than private firms, which have to balance the preferences of consumers for both newer, more innovative products and low prices. This leads them, in order to satisfy their customers, to offer broad formularies that have a wide selection of both new medicines and generics. In contrast, the federal government faces intense political pressures to control costs, but does not have customers. Therefore, political incentives to achieve budget savings are powerful, while incentives to satisfy consumer preferences for more-inclusive formularies are relatively weak. The dissatisfaction of some patients who lose access to their preferred drugs would be offset by the support of other constituencies concerned more about lower prices, or that would benefit from increased spending in their favored programs.

The Expected Outcome Is Grim

Accordingly the most likely outcome we can expect from adopting the VA model for Medicare would be the following: substantially lower prices, smaller formularies, and reduced revenues from pharmaceutical sales. The capital market would view investment in pharmaceutical research and development less favorably, and fewer new medicines would be developed.

Based on a review of existing government purchasing programs, new research from the Manhattan Institute provides specific estimates of these effects: Prices would be driven down by over 35 percent by 2025. The cumulative decline in drug R&D for 2007–2025 would be about $196 billion in year 2005 dollars, or $10.3 billion per year. Because R&D costs for new medicines are about $1 billion, the loss would be about 196 new drugs. Other published research reports findings that each pharmaceutical R&D investment of roughly $2000 yields an expected gain of one life-year. Accordingly, an annual R&D decline of $10 billion would result in an expected loss of 5 million life-years each year. If we assume, again conservatively, the value of a life-year at $100,000, the economic cost of this effect would be about $500 billion per year, far in excess of total U.S. spending on pharmaceuticals.

It is difficult to predict which drugs will fail to be developed as a result of government price negotiations, but it seems clear that Congress is wading into dangerous waters. As the experience in Canada and Europe shows, government mandated drug formularies and interference in drug pricing leads to substantially less drug innovation and rationing of access to the new medicines that do come to market. Thus, would Ms. Pelosi's politically attractive but ill-considered idea have as its unintended consequence an increase in future human suffering.

Periodical Bibliography

The following articles have been selected to supplement the diverse views presented in this chapter.

Doug Bandow — "Prescription Drug Price Controls Are Coming, Sooner or Later," *Examiner*, May 3, 2007.

Chain Drug Review — "PhRMA Works to Change Perceptions on Rx Spending," August 20, 2007.

Chicago Tribune — "A Medicare Gamble?" December 3, 2006.

Greg D'Angelo — "Why the New Congress Should Not Fix Drug Prices," *Heritage Foundation WebMemo*, December 1, 2006. www.heritage.org.

Samuel Garten and R. Victor Falkner — "Now Is the Time for Price Controls on Prescription Drugs," *Good Health*, 2005. http://goodhealth.freeservers.com.

Alan Goldhammer — Statement at the House Committee on Energy and Commerce Hearing on the Food and Drug Import Safety Act, September 26, 2007.

Deroy Murdock — "A Price Control Virus," *National Review Online*, January 2, 2007.

Pfizer — "Prescription Drug Importation." www.pfizer.com.

Peter Pitts — "First, Do No Harm to Seniors," *Chicago Tribune*, April 24, 2007.

Senior Journal — "Consumers Union Urges Passage of Price Negotiation for Medicare Drugs," January 12, 2007.

Billy Tauzin — Remarks at PhRMA Annual Meeting, March 16, 2007. www.phrma.org.

David Vitter — "Continuing the Fight for Reimportation of Prescription Drugs," December 8, 2006. http://vitter.senate.gov.

For Further Discussion

Chapter 1

1. The author of the first viewpoint, Jan Jarboe Russell, presents one long, detailed story of someone she knows to support her point that clinical drug trials save lives. David Evans, Michael Smith, and Liz Willen, on the other hand, use several shorter facts and quotes from various sources to illustrate their argument that drug trials endanger people. Which style do you find more convincing? Why?

2. In viewpoint four, Ronald Bailey devotes much time to explaining and sometimes conceding his opponents' views. Does this hurt or help his argument, in your opinion? How so?

3. What type of evidence does Iain Chalmers use to bolster his claim that clinical trials registration is needed? What type does International Federation of Pharmaceutical Manufacturers & Associations use in the opposing viewpoint? Which evidence do you find more persuasive?

4. Reread the viewpoints in this chapter. Which policies governing pharmaceutical research and development do you think are working, and which need to be adjusted? Explain, citing facts from the viewpoints.

Chapter 2

1. Henry I. Miller lays blame on federal regulators for patients' deaths. Miller insists deaths are caused by drug delays. Do you agree? Why? Support your answer, citing the text.

2. Scott Ballenger and Ralph W. Moss both discuss the implications of the *Abigail* case. If you were the judge, would you side with patients who want access to potentially dan-

gerous medicines, or would you rule in favor of the Food and Drug Administration (FDA), whose job is to protect patients from such drugs? Explain.

3. How does Rick Kellerman's view about the role of pharmacists affect his opinions about behind-the-counter drugs?

4. Several viewpoints in this chapter discuss the need to get drugs approved quickly while still guaranteeing safety. How might this balance best be achieved, in your opinion? Do you think there should be more laws to ensure drug safety, or fewer barriers to drug approval? Why?

5. A major portion of this chapter discusses conflicts of interest within the medical community. For the most part, both sides agree that such conflicts exist but they differ over whether these conflicts are harmful or benign. What do you think? Citing the texts, develop your answer.

Chapter 3

1. The Pharmaceutical Research and Manufacturers of America is an organization of U.S. pharmaceutical research and biotechnology companies. How might this be influencing its opinion that drug representatives ought to be able to have informative discussions with doctors?

2. Several of the authors in this chapter contend that pharmaceutical marketers are a powerful and influential force on doctors and patients. Do you agree or disagree with this assessment? Present evidence from the viewpoints to support your answer.

Chapter 4

1. Richard A. Epstein is a senior fellow at the Hoover Institution, which promotes free society with limited governmental intrusion, and he works as a consultant for pharmaceuti-

cal companies. How might the author's background credentials inform his opinion on the cost of drugs in America?

2. Reread viewpoint four's opening paragraph. In arguing that prescription drug importation would expose Americans to dangerous medications, Michelle Plasari paints a picture of sick children and dying pets. What method of argument is she using, and is it effective? Explain.

3. In viewpoints five and six, National Committee to Preserve Social Security and Medicare and Benjamin Zycher each compare price negotiation plans for Medicare drugs to the system used by the Department of Veterans Affairs (VA). However, they draw vastly different conclusions about the success of the VA's drug program and what this would spell for Medicare. With whom do you agree? Explain.

Organizations to Contact

The editors have compiled the following list of organizations concerned with the issues debated in this book. The descriptions are derived from materials provided by the organizations. All have publications or information available for interested readers. The list was compiled on the date of publication of the present volume; the information provided here may change. Be aware that many organizations take several weeks or longer to respond to inquiries, so allow as much time as possible.

American Medical Association (AMA)
515 N. State Street, Chicago, IL   60610
(800) 621-8335
Web site: www.ama-assn.org/

The American Medical Association (AMA) is the largest professional association for medical doctors. It helps set standards for medical education and practices and is a powerful lobby in Washington for physicians' interests. The association publishes journals for many medical fields, including the monthly *Archives of Surgery* and the weekly *Journal of the American Medical Association.*

Center for Drug Evaluation and Research
Food and Drug Administration, Rockville, MD   20857
(301) 827-4573
e-mail: druginfo@fda.hhs.gov
Web site: www.fda.gov/cder

The Center for Drug Evaluation and Research promotes and protects the health of Americans by assuring that prescription and over-the-counter drugs are safe and effective. The center routinely monitors TV, radio, and print advertisements to see that they are truthful and balanced. It publishes the *News Along the Pike* newsletter as well as various reports.

The Heritage Foundation
214 Massachusetts Avenue NE, Washington, DC   20002-4999
(202) 546-4400 • fax: (202) 546-8328
e-mail: info@heritage.org
Web site: www.heritage.org

The Heritage Foundation is a public policy research institute that advocates limited government and the free market system. It believes the private sector, not the government, should be relied upon to solve social problems. It publishes the quarterly *Policy Review* as well as monographs, books, and background papers explaining its stance on health care and Medicare reform, prescription drug cost controls, and drug importation.

Institute of Medicine (IOM)
500 Fifth Street NW, Washington, DC   20001
(202) 334-2352 • fax: (202) 334-1412
e-mail: iomwww@nas.edu
Web site: www.iom.edu

The Institute of Medicine (IOM) serves as an independent scientific advisor to policy makers, professionals, community leaders, and the public. It strives to provide information on biomedical science, medicine, and health that is unbiased and grounded in science. Its many reports on health care and prescription drugs are available on the Web site.

National Association of Boards of Pharmacy (NABP)
1600 Feehanville Drive, Mount Prospect, IL   60056
(847) 391-4406 • fax: (847) 391-4502
e-mail: custserv@nabp.net
Web site: www.nabp.net

The National Association of Boards of Pharmacy (NABP) is a professional association that represents the state boards of pharmacy in all fifty states, eight Canadian provinces, and other countries. It assists its members in the development and enforcement of uniform standards of care to help protect public health. It publishes the *NABP Newsletter*, state newsletters in thirty-four states, and *National Pharmacy Compliance News*.

National Center for Policy Analysis (NCPA)

601 Pennsylvania Avenue NW, Suite 900 South Building
Washington, DC   20004
(202) 220-3082 • fax: (202) 220-3096
e-mail: ncpa@ncpa.org
Web site: www.ncpa.org

The National Center for Policy Analysis (NCPA) is a nonprofit public policy research institute that aims to develop and promote alternatives to government regulation and control. It prints a bimonthly newsletter, numerous health care policy studies, such as *Who Pays Higher Prices for Prescription Drugs?* and commentaries including "Time, Money and the Market for Drugs." Its Web site includes a section on health under which its studies, policy backgrounders, and brief analyses can be found.

National Institutes of Health

9000 Rockville Pike, Bethesda, MD   20892
(301) 496-4000
e-mail: nihinfo@od.nih.gov
Web site: www.nih.gov

Part of the U.S. Department of Health and Human Services, the National Institutes of Health (NIH) include the National Human Genome Research Institute and the National Cancer Institute. Their mission is to discover knowledge that will improve the nation's health. They do so by conducting and supporting research, training research investigators, and helping disburse medical information. The NIH also publish online fact sheets, brochures, and handbooks.

National Pharmaceutical Council (NPC)
1894 Preston White Drive, Reston, VA   20191
(703) 620-6390 • fax: (703) 476-0904
Web site: http://npcnow.org

Supported by more than twenty of the nation's major research-based pharmaceutical companies, the National Pharmaceutical Council (NPC) sponsors research and education projects aimed at demonstrating the appropriate use of medicines to improve health outcomes. It focuses on the use of evidence-based medicine to help patients make the best, most cost-effective health care decisions. Monographs on disease management, newsletters, and other publications geared toward policy makers, health care providers, employers, and consumers are available on its Web site.

Pharmaceutical Research and Manufacturers of America (PhRMA)
1100 Fifteenth Street NW, Washington, DC   20005
(202) 835-3400 • fax: (202) 835-3434
Web site: www.phrma.org

The Pharmaceutical Research and Manufacturers of America (PhRMA) represents U.S. drug research and biotechnology companies. It advocates public policies that encourage discovery of important medicines and its medical officers sometimes testify before Congress on issues such as drug advertising, safety, and importation. Among its publications are *Why Do Medicines Cost So Much?* and *PhRMA Guiding Principles Direct to Consumer Advertisements About Prescription Medicines.*

World Health Organization (WHO)
Avenue Appia 20, Geneva 27   CH - 1211
   Switzerland
e-mail: info@who.int
Web site: www.who.int

World Health Organization (WHO) has been operating its International Drug Monitoring Programme since 1968. *The World Health Report* is published by WHO annually and its pharmaceuticals newsletter is distributed six times a year. There is a page on its Web site for pharmaceutical products which offers fact sheets, technical information, and information on related WHO programs and activities.

Bibliography of Books

John Abramson — *Overdosed America: The Broken Promise of American Medicine.* New York: HarperCollins, 2004.

Marcia Angell — *The Truth About the Drug Companies: How They Deceive Us and What To Do About It.* New York: Random House, 2004.

Jerry Avorn — *Powerful Medicines: The Benefits, Risks, and Costs of Prescription Drugs.* New York: Knopf, 2004.

Alison Bass — *Side Effects: A Prosecutor, a Whistle-blower, and a Bestselling Antidepressant on Trial.* Chapel Hill, NC: Algonquin, 2008.

Mark H. Beers — *The Merck Manual of Medical Information* (2nd ed.). New York: Pocket, 2003.

Howard Brody — *Hooked: Ethics, the Medical Profession, and the Pharmaceutical Industry.* Lanham, MD: Rowman and Littlefield, 2007.

Jay S. Cohen — *Overdose: The Case Against the Drug Companies.* New York: Penguin Putnam, 2001.

Greg Critser — *Generation Rx: How Prescription Drugs Are Altering American Lives, Minds, and Bodies.* New York: Houghton Mifflin, 2005.

Lawrence H. Diller	*Should I Medicate My Child? Sane Solutions for Troubled Kids with—& Without—Psychiatric Drugs.* New York: Basic, 2003.
Carl Elliott and Peter D. Kramer	*Better than Well: American Medicine Meets the American Dream.* New York: W.W. Norton, 2004.
Richard Epstein	*Overdose: How Excessive Government Regulation Stifles Pharmaceutical Innovation.* New Haven, CT: Yale University Press, 2006.
Stan Finkelstein and Peter Temin	*Reasonable Rx: Solving the Drug Price Crisis.* Upper Saddle River, NJ: FT Press, 2008.
Michael C. Gerald	*The Complete Idiot's Guide to Prescription Drugs.* New York: Alpha, 2006.
Kenneth Getz and Deborah Borfitz	*Informed Consent: The Consumer's Guide to the Risks and Benefits of Volunteering for Clinical Trials.* Boston, MA: CenterWatch, 2002.
Merrill Goozner	*The $800 Million Pill: The Truth Behind the Cost of New Drugs.* Berkeley and Los Angeles: University of California Press, 2004.
Katharine Greider	*The Big Fix: How the Pharmaceutical Industry Rips off American Consumers.* New York: Public Affairs, 2003.

Fran Hawthorne   *Inside the FDA: The Business and Politics Behind the Drugs We Take and the Food We Eat.* Hoboken, NJ: Wiley, 2005.

David Healy   *Let Them Eat Prozac: The Unhealthy Relationship Between the Pharmaceutical Industry and Depression.* New York: New York University Press, 2006.

Philip J. Hilts   *Protecting America's Health: The FDA, Business, and One Hundred Years of Regulation.* Chapel Hill: University of North Carolina Press, 2004.

Institute of Medicine Committee on the Assessment of the U.S. Drug Safety System   *The Future of Drug Safety: Promoting and Protecting the Health of the Public.* Washington, DC: National Academies Press, 2007.

Jerome P. Kassirer   *On the Take: How Medicine's Complicity with Big Business Can Endanger Your Health.* New York: Oxford University Press, 2005.

Henry I. Miller   *To America's Health: A Proposal to Reform the Food and Drug Administration.* Stanford, CA: Hoover Institution Press, 2000.

Carole Moussalli   *Vault Career Guide to Pharmaceuticals Sales & Marketing.* New York: Vault, Inc., 2006.

Ray Moynihan and Alan Cassels — *Selling Sickness: How the World's Pharmaceutical Companies Are Turning Us All into Patients.* New York: Nation, 2005.

David G. Nathan — *The Cancer Treatment Revolution: How Smart Drugs and Other New Therapies are Renewing Our Hope and Changing the Face of Medicine.* Hoboken, NJ: Wiley, 2007.

Rick Ng — *Drugs—From Discovery to Approval.* Hoboken, NJ: Wiley, 2004.

Melody Petersen — *Our Daily Meds: How the Pharmaceutical Companies Transformed Themselves into Slick Marketing Machines and Hooked the Nation on Prescription Drugs.* New York: Farrar, Straus and Giroux, 2008.

Drew Pinsky — *When Painkillers Become Dangerous: What Everyone Needs to Know About OxyContin and Other Prescription Drugs.* Center City, MN: Hazelden, 2004.

Reader's Digest Editors — *Reader's Digest Guide to Drugs and Supplements: Prescription Drugs.* Pleasantville, NY: Reader's Digest, 2002.

Thompson PDR — *The PDR Pocket Guide to Prescription Drugs* (8th ed.). New York: Pocket, 2007.

Andrea Tone and Elizabeth Watkins — *Medicating Modern America: Prescription Drugs in History.* New York: New York University Press, 2007.

Ben A. Williams — *Surviving Terminal Cancer: Clinical Trials, Drug Cocktails, and Other Treatments Your Oncologist Won't Tell You About.* Minneapolis, MN: Fairview Press, 2002.

Jane Williams — *Insider's Guide to the World of Pharmaceutical Sales* (8th ed.). Arlington, TX: Principle Publications, 2005.

Sid M. Wolfe — *Worst Pills, Best Pills: A Consumer's Guide to Avoiding Drug-Induced Death or Illness.* New York: Pocket, 2005.

Index